Is Globalization Over?

Is Globalization Over?

Jeremy Green

polity

First published in 2019 by Polity Press

Polity Press
65 Bridge Street
Cambridge CB2 1UR, UK

101 Station Landing
Suite 300
Medford, MA 02155, USA

ISBN-13: 978-1-5095-3544-6 (hardback)
ISBN-13: 978-1-5095-3545-3 (paperback)

A catalogue record for this book is available from the British Library.

Library of Congress Cataloging-in-Publication Data
Names: Green, Jeremy, 1985- author.
Title: Is globalization over? / Jeremy Green.
Other titles: Is globalisation over?
Description: Medford, MA : Polity Press, [2019] | Includes bibliographical references.
Identifiers: LCCN 2019014887 (print) | LCCN 2019017628 (ebook) | ISBN 9781509535460 (Epub) | ISBN 9781509535446 (hardback) | ISBN 9781509535453 (pbk.)
Subjects: LCSH: International economic relations. | International economic integration. | Neoliberalism.
Classification: LCC HF1359 (ebook) | LCC HF1359 .G7244 2019 (print) | DDC 337--dc23
LC record available at https://lccn.loc.gov/2019014887

Typeset in 11 on 14 pt Sabon by
Servis Filmsetting Ltd, Stockport, Cheshire
Printed and bound in Great Britain by CPI Group (UK) Ltd, Croydon

For further information on Polity, visit our website: politybooks.com

Contents

Acknowledgements

I have built up a number of debts of gratitude during the writing of this book. George Owers at Polity has provided consistent encouragement and engagement with the project. His editorial input was rigorous and honest, and forced me to sharpen or expand the arguments at several points in the book. I must also thank the reviewers of the book and everyone involved in the project at Polity for their time, effort and support. At Jesus College, Duncan Kelly has provided a constant source of intellectual curiosity and encouragement. And teaching my students at Jesus and Cambridge more broadly has been stimulating and inspiring. My family have offered their support and encouragement too. Finally, I have to express my deepest thanks to Solène. We met while I was writing this book. Since then, the inspiration, determination and warmth that you bring have only deepened my commitment to wrestle with the problems that are the subject of this book.

Preface

I began writing this book in the summer of 2018. It was an unusual summer in England. The English football team performed well in a major tournament. Weeks of endless sunshine sapped the grass of its colour. An unbreaking wave of heat slowed the normal pace of life. Shops across London sold out of fans as the high temperatures became unbearable. The weather was a daily challenge to my writing rhythms. But more than this, the extreme conditions offered a constant reminder of the deep changes going on in the world. The changing climate, more unstable, unpredictable, and extreme in its patterns than before, mirrored the sense of a political and economic world in flux.

All around us, the old certainties, from the comforting inconsistency of English summers to the onwards march of a more integrated world economy and the global ascendancy of liberal democracy, have seemed to give way over the past decade. The Global Financial Crisis of 2007/8 marked a turning point in the world economy. It signalled the end of a triumphant period of Western expansionism and shook confidence in the globalization project. Ten years after that crisis began, the political consequences are only now coming more fully into vision. From the rise of Donald Trump to Brexit and the deepening trade war between China and the US, global politics after the crisis looks and feels very different. And underlying all of these changes we can hear the quickening, deepening drumbeat of climate crisis. It is a sound that still seems all too inaudible to many of the world's political leaders. But it is one that we will have to heed much more sharply if we are to salvage a positive future for our species on this planet. How we deal with the crisis of the world economy will be central to our prospects for tackling climate change. We can no longer credibly think about these two dominant problems of our age in anything other than the deepest of unions.

This book is my attempt to make sense of these changing times – to try to gain a stronger foothold on a terrain that is shifting rapidly beneath our feet. While this has proved a cathartic effort in some respects, offering greater clarity where once there was only ambiguity, it has proved to be unsettling in others. It has forced me to look unflinchingly at the precariousness of our global condition. In writing this book my hope has been that it might offer the reader a clearer guide to understanding our times. I have aimed to do this by unearthing a deeper history of the ebbs and flows of the globalisation project, to show how the ideas and institutions that have guided it have developed, and to indicate how we might hope to change them for the better in the future. Knowing how to interpret the political and economic world of today is a matter of importance not only for specialists – it is vital for everyone. In an age when

Preface

our faith in democracy has been shaken and ominous political forces are rising to the fore, a proper sense of the fault lines and pressure points within the global economy can help us apply our collective energies more effectively to push for a better future.

1

The crisis of globalization

The collapse of the Berlin Wall on 9 November 1989 heralded the beginning of a new era for the global economy. The political disintegration of the Soviet Union that followed symbolized the defeat of socialist alternatives to market capitalism. New spaces opened for the untrammelled expansion of globalizing markets previously confined by Cold War divisions.[1] The post-Second World War contest between American capitalism and Soviet communism had split the world economy into rival geographical spheres of influence shaped by competing visions of political economy. As the Cold War ended, the former Soviet economies were subjected to the 'shock therapy' of rapid pro-market reforms and sudden exposure to the competitive forces of global capitalism. The age of globalization had arrived. Western liberals triumphantly pronounced the victory of free-market capitalism and its political handmaiden – liberal democracy.[2]

Globalization became the new buzzword of the social sciences, with vigorous discussion about its meaning, origins, and effects. Some saw the onset of globalization as an epochal shift towards a 'borderless world'.[3] Traditional boundaries between nation states would dissolve under the pressure of an increasingly technologically sophisticated and networked form of global economic integration, bringing the possibility of enhanced prosperity to the world. Others were more circumspect, suggesting that the globalization debate was an intellectual variant of the Emperor's new clothes – we had been here before, with an international economy in the late nineteenth century that was equally, perhaps even more, interconnected and cosmopolitan than that of the 1990s.[4] For radical critics of globalization, this new era represented the aggressive extension of capitalism into untapped frontiers. Exploitative economic practices were now intensified in pursuit of profit and an ascendant transnational capitalist class was empowered at the expense of workers.[5] These critics viewed globalization as a sharply polarized story of winners and losers.

This book does not replay the well-worn contest between rival interpretations of globalization. Instead, it offers a way of thinking about globalization tailored to rapidly changing times. You do not have to search far or hard today to hear talk about the end of globalization. The term 'deglobalization' has begun to enter the popular lexicon.[6] If globalization was the zeitgeist of the 1990s, then it is its antonym, deglobalization, that captures the troubled spirit of today. But how can we make sense of whether globalization really is over? This book explores the contemporary crisis of the world economy. It does so by adopting a longer view of globalization – thinking about its past, present, and future.

To do this the book makes a simple but important distinction – between globalization as a *process* and a *condition*. As a process globalization involves the widening, deepening, acceleration, and intensification of cross-border flows of goods, capital, people, and ideas. Over time, the cumulative effects of these globalization processes, through increasing the volume, intensity, breadth, and depth of flows that connect different countries, transform the very background circumstances, institutions, networks, and norms within which modern capitalism exists. Globalization becomes increasingly 'sticky' as these processes bring about a more pervasive globalized *condition* – a context of increased economic and political interconnection and interdependence. The globalized condition is a context that transforms the way we think about and organize our political, economic, and cultural ways of life. Our assumptions about what is possible, about what we can eat or wear, how we can travel, or what sort of employment we can find, are remoulded by the gradual deepening of the globalized condition.

The processes that propel globalization and the condition that they gradually bring about are tightly interlinked. Globalizing processes are the drivers of the globalized condition. Without the former, the latter cannot exist. Once a certain degree of globalization is reached, though, reversing the processes that drive globalization becomes more difficult. Over time, the deepening of the globalized condition raises the costs and increases the obstacles to curbing the processes at the heart of globalization. The more pervasive reach of the globalized condition, the way it structures and moulds our lives, makes undoing globalization harder. It makes the behaviours, interests, and habits of thought of more and more people, businesses, states, and other organizations increasingly dependent on a globalized economy. These two faces of globalization are not identical, and a partial or even substantial decline in the continued development of globalization processes will still leave us living within a deeply globalized way of life. This is not least because the economic processes at the heart of globalization – in terms of increased international trade, investment, and labour flows between countries – also leave a deep cultural imprint that changes the way that we interpret our world and reshapes our expectations of what everyday life looks like.

Contemporary globalization has deep historical roots. It has experienced previous periods of crisis and even reversal. But an important distinguishing feature of this current crisis of globalization is that it is occurring within a much more pervasive globalized condition than ever experienced before. That buys globalization time. But it also raises the costs of a potential collapse of globalization should it occur, and it has carried in its wake environmental degradation that gravely threatens the future of humanity as a species.

As a *process* of deepening and widening of societal interconnection, through flows of trade, capital, and labour, it does indeed appear that globalization has stalled. It has perhaps even reversed. World trade as a share of world gross domestic product (GDP), which tracks the value of trade as a percentage of the overall economic output of the world economy, fell from around 61 per cent in 2008 to 52 per cent in 2009. By 2016, it was still some five per cent lower than its pre-crisis peak.[7] During the gradual economic recovery after the crisis, between 2012 and 2014, annual global trade growth averaged 3.4 per cent annually. That is less than half of the pre-crisis growth rate of around seven per cent per year. Looking at global net foreign direct investment (FDI) inflows, a measure for assessing flows of longer-term investment across borders, the story of decline is similar. Those flows peaked at just over five per cent of world GDP in 2008, before falling dramatically to just over two per cent in 2009. By 2016, they were still only three per cent of world GDP.[8]

Added to these declining trade and capital flows, the wider politics of free trade look more unstable than they have done for decades. Stalled free trade deals, from the Transatlantic Trade and Investment Partnership (TTIP), to the EU–Canada Comprehensive Economic and Trade Agreement (CETA), and the Trans-Pacific Partnership (TPP), signal a major roadblock in the journey towards trade liberalization. Donald Trump has embarked on a nascent trade war with China, raising tariffs on all $500 billions of Chinese imports coming into the United States.[9] And the movement of people around the world is likely to become more difficult as Western politics takes on a more sharply anti-immigrant tenor in response to the populist tide sweeping through the West.

Yet, as a condition, a way of life shaped by a high level of political–economic interdependence and integration, globalization remains just as enveloping and entrenched as ever. Returning to the example of trade, the figure for world trade as a share of world GDP was 24 per cent in 1960. That was a period in which the booming post-war international economy had already reached a higher level of globalization than the early years after the Second World War. Returning to that greatly diminished figure would require that the value of world trade as a percentage of world GDP collapse much further, to less than half its current level. A decline of that magnitude would entail the complete reorganization of the global economy.

In surveying the trade policy response to the financial crisis, the World Trade Organization (WTO) found that tariff and non-tariff barriers to free trade did increase, as domestic producers looked for government support against foreign competition during the recession. But the multilateral trade rules put in place by the WTO over previous decades continued to act as a 'bulwark' against the outbreak of wholesale protectionism in the immediate aftermath of the financial crisis.[10] This prevented a recurrence of the dramatic shift to protectionism witnessed during the Great Depression of the 1930s. The singular trade power of the United States still threatens the world with a more strident turn to protectionism, but contemporary trade disputes are occurring within a much more rules-based trade order governed by international organizations like the WTO. By 2008, the WTO had 153 member-countries and accounted for almost 100 per cent of international trade.[11] Even with US support for the WTO in doubt under the leadership of President Trump, there is still major support for the current international trade system from within economic superpowers like the European Union (EU) and China.

Similarly, if we look again at the measure of net global FDI inflows, the current level of three per cent of world GDP is still six times the value for 1970, when net global FDI inflows were just 0.5 per cent of world GDP. To get back to a genuinely deglobalized world, then, would involve nothing less than a complete transformation of contemporary corporate strategy and global production processes, disrupting complex global supply-chains at huge economic and political cost. That is not impossible, but it would be a very tough project to achieve without leading to a collapse of domestic political support for whichever leader tried to advance that kind of policy agenda. If it were to occur in a sudden, disorderly, and beggar-thy-neighbour context it would likely have catastrophic consequences for the global economy.

How did we come to live in such an interconnected world economy? The globalized condition is a consequence of decades of cumulative globalization processes that gradually connected the world economy, transforming the way that our political institutions and economic models operate. It is also a product of technological innovations, from modern transportation to the internet, that have shrunk space by compressing the time it takes to travel from one country to another and enabled us to communicate in real time all over the world. It has been built into the very fabric of contemporary capitalism. It is embedded within our cultures and habits of consumption. It is represented by the clothes that we wear, produced in South Asian countries such as Bangladesh within the supply-chains of huge Multinational Corporations like Nike. It is embodied by the iPhones that have become so integral to individual identity and communication and which are assembled in China, drawing on components made across a vast range of countries, including Japan, South Korea, Taiwan, Singapore, Switzerland, and the Netherlands.[12] The iPhone is just one example of the huge range of products that find their way to us through a vast web of

7

complex supply-chains that criss-cross the globe.[13] And our globalized condition also manifests itself in the ease with which we can travel around the world through a vast network of flights and airports that fuel a massive global tourism industry. These features of contemporary globalization are more intimately connected to our personal lives and the organization of our societies than ever before.

Globalization then and now

Modern globalization has occurred in two major waves. The first from 1870 to 1914, and the second from 1945 to today. These waves mark out the two broad epochs within which the modern industrialized world economy has been characterized by consistent growth in flows of trade, capital, and people across borders. The first wave was ended by the disruption caused by the First World War. After failed attempts to restore an open and interconnected international economy during the 1920s, and the disastrous turn to rival projects of national economic autarky during the 1930s, globalization was gradually relaunched under the auspices of American international leadership after the Second World War.

Beyond these two broad waves of globalization, though, we can also identify more discrete eras linked to the rise and fall of different liberal doctrines of political economy. These doctrines have provided the roadmaps for globalization. They have been used to justify changes in the rules, priorities, and institutions that govern the international economy. The transition between these ruling doctrines of liberal economic ideas has frequently occurred in the wake of international economic crises, from the Great Depression of the 1930s, through the international economic turmoil of the 1970s, to the 2007/8 Global Financial Crisis. These crises have taken different forms and had different effects. But on each occasion they have eroded popular support for globalization, undermined international economic stability, and opened spaces for alternative ways of thinking about how best to govern economies, both domestically and internationally.

Much like today's world economy the first wave of globalization, which spanned the *belle époque* from 1870 to 1914, was also characterized by increased levels of international trade, growth in cross-border capital flows, and the mass movement of populations. It was underpinned by technological innovations like the telegraph and the steam ship, which shrank the world by making it easier to travel and communicate over large distances. Describing this highly interconnected pre-First-World-War international economy, John Maynard Keynes famously noted that:

> the inhabitant of London could order by telephone, sipping his morning tea in bed, the various products of the whole earth, in such quantity as he might see fit, and reasonably expect their early delivery upon his doorstep; he could at the same moment and by the same means adventure his wealth in the natural resources and new enterprises of any quarter of the world, and share, without exertion or even trouble, in their prospective fruits and advantages ... He could secure forthwith, if he wished it, cheap and comfortable means of transit to any country or climate without passport or formality, could dispatch his servant to the neighbouring office of

a bank for such supply of the precious metals as might seem convenient.[14]

Keynes' statement has often been taken as evidence that this earlier period of globalization was comparable to today. But Keynes prefaced this description by recognizing that the fruits of globalization primarily applied to 'any man of capacity or character at all exceeding the average'. This was a narrow vision of nineteenth-century globalization written from the perspective of affluent male metropolitan London elites. The sort of people that would have the resources to dispatch their 'servant' on errands.

Although still clearly uneven in its effects, with some benefiting much more than others, today's globalization is much more universal and enveloping in its reach than ever before. Since 1945, and especially since the end of the Cold War, the world has moved towards a much deeper form of international economic connectivity. The condition of globalization has much deeper and broader roots now than it did then. This means, as we shall see in Chapter 3, that comparisons to the breakdown of the first wave of modern globalization are inaccurate.

In today's economy, stocks and shares can be traded online from the comfort of a rural home, or on the move via an app on a smartphone. Many more people participate in and depend upon global financial markets than they did during the first wave of globalization, whether it be through individual investments or participation in vast collective pension funds. And, geographically, it is not just top-rank global cities like London that are the networked hubs of the world economy. Many other cities have joined the ranks of a much wider and denser 'world city network', stretching from Los Angeles, via Chicago and Toronto, to New York, and on to London and Paris, via Berlin and Moscow, to Sydney, Shanghai, and Tokyo.[15] Airports connect even second and third-tier cities within individual countries to many different parts of the globe.

Travelling abroad no longer requires the dispatch of servants to attain precious metals. We can exchange paper currency at the airport, use an internationally accepted bank card in a foreign cash machine, or make electronic payments without any recourse to currency at all. And our habits of consumption and ways of life are much more intimately globalized than they were before. It would not be uncommon for an individual in the United Kingdom today to awake in a Swedish-designed bed, put on clothing made in Bangladesh or Indonesia, drink morning coffee produced in Colombia and purchased from an American-owned company, read the international news on a phone produced by workers in China using materials from the Congo, within a supply-chain coordinated by an American corporation, before driving to work in a German or Japanese-designed car produced in Britain.

To say that globalization processes have stalled or partially reversed is not, then, to say that the globalized condition will simply unravel. This is the basic conflation that those heralding deglobalization have made. They have confused the slowing and partial reversal of globalization processes with a wider unravelling of the globalized condition. It is this confused position that this book seeks to redress. The globalized condition has been built up over decades of previous economic

11

integration. It is written into the fabric of modern political and economic institutions, international organizations, business strategies, and ways of life. The depth of the globalized condition, by hugely increasing the penalties associated with renouncing interdependence and transforming our experiences of everyday life, acts as an important force for continuity. It gives contemporary globalization much greater staying power than the first wave of globalization that ended with the catastrophe of two world wars.

The pervasiveness of the contemporary globalized condition should not, though, be a cause for complacency. Make no mistake about it – globalization is in crisis. And the bad news is that with more and more of our way of life now configured around the background assumptions of a highly globalized economy, the disruption caused by a complete breakdown of globalization would be more devastating than ever before. It would force us to fundamentally reconfigure our political and economic systems, our cultural coordinates, in a way that would have the possibility of generating significant conflict.

Confidence in the continued momentum of global economic integration has been deeply shaken over the last decade. In 2017, the influential international journal *Foreign Affairs* asked a number of experts to answer the question, 'Will Economic Globalization End?'[16] Such a question would have appeared almost unthinkable a decade earlier. Politics within the West and in many developing countries had become about how to manage the effects of economic globalization and harness its benefits. But the trajectory of the process itself felt secure. It was almost unquestionable. That sentiment was embodied by Margaret Thatcher's famous slogan that, 'there is no alternative' to international free-market capitalism.

So what accounts for this sudden turnaround in the fortunes of globalization? The current crisis of globalization is, in part, a legacy of the 2007/8 Global Financial Crisis. The crisis first broke out in August 2007 when the French bank, BNP Paribas, announced that its operations were paralysed by a liquidity crisis in which the inter-bank lending at the heart of the global financial system was freezing up. A run on the British bank Northern Rock in September 2007, by depositors fearing the loss of their savings, marked a deepening of the crisis and triggered a global collapse of confidence in the financial system.[17] Inter-bank lending markets froze during the 'credit crunch' that followed. The collapse of the major US investment bank, Lehman Brothers, in September 2008 led to intensified global panic. The US and UK governments were forced to step in with huge bailout packages and the nationalization or mergers of their ailing banks.

What began as a financial crisis soon morphed into a wider recession in the West and a slowing of growth globally. Trade volumes collapsed in the immediate aftermath of the crisis and capital flows dropped sharply too. In the Eurozone economies, the credit crunch and the recession that followed provoked a broader sovereign debt crisis from 2010, bringing economic ruin to Greece and pitting debtor and creditor nations against one another in the toxic austerity politics that followed. The crisis led to the longest and deepest recession that the advanced Western economies had faced since the Second World War.[18] Wages stagnated and living standards plateaued or decreased in the decade of slower growth that has followed.

The financial crisis lifted the lid on a series of deep and long-standing problems within the Western political economies and superimposed new problems upon them. In doing so it transformed the political landscape in those countries. These were the countries that had been the driving force of the globalization project. That project had relied upon a stable domestic political consensus in favour of economic openness, freer markets, and a rules-based international trading system. In the decade since the financial crisis, that consensus has begun to unravel under the strains of contemporary economic, social, and cultural transformation within these countries. Internationally, Western economies can no longer be so sure of their continuing political and economic dominance in the face of rapid economic catch-up by the emerging markets of Asia and Africa. Slow economic growth, deepening inequality, and austerity have weakened social solidarity and revealed more starkly the polarized fortunes of different social groups and classes under contemporary globalization. Increased levels of migration, themselves partly linked to the uneven effects of globalization, have generated nativist resentment and populist politics from the host populations.

The events of 2007/8 also illuminated the gradual, longer-term transformations that had been underway within the accelerated globalization that set in after the Cold War. Most notably, the crisis revealed the magnitude of China's rise to pre-eminence and the shift of economic and political power from West to East.[19] This new period of post-crisis politics has proved threatening to the very foundations of globalization. It has unsettled the West's self-image as the undisputed leader and primary beneficiary of globalization, straining the internal politics and economics of the European Union and transforming the United States' approach to managing the world economy under President Donald Trump. And it has shaken popular democratic confidence in the ability of a globalized economy to deliver economic and social security.

Globalization's wider travails cannot, though, be reduced to the effects of the financial crisis alone. Many of the issues that animate the contemporary politics of backlash against globalization have much deeper roots. They stretch back decades and, as this book shows, are linked with the earlier historical origins of the globalization project and a consistent tension within it. The tension is between, on the one hand, the project of liberal universalism that seeks to dissolve national boundaries to the movements of goods and capital within an integrated system of global trade and production. And on the other, the territorially based political representation and sovereign authority of the nation state.

Acting as a catalyst, the crisis intensified the political manifestation of these deep and long-standing underlying tensions within the globalization project. It combined the aggravation of existing problems with new political and economic challenges unique to its immediate effects. But the liberal rules-based order that provided the political casing for the globalization project had already begun to run into trouble, a victim of its own post-Cold War hubris. American leaders and their Western allies overextended and intensified globalization with the demise of the Soviet Union, increasing the number of state players involved and enabling emerging markets to catch up with the advanced Western economies.[20] Under George W. Bush the liberal project began to morph once again, as it has throughout different moments since the Second World War, into a more nakedly imperialist mission, unseating Saddam Hussein under false pretences and destabilizing the entire Middle East region.[21] Domestically, the shift towards a more aggressively market-liberal political economy led to increased polarization of wealth and income, weakening the legitimacy of globalizing capitalism at its core.[22]

Within democratic politics, the popular revolts against elite consensus in Anglo-America, through Britain's vote for Brexit and the election of Donald Trump in the United States, have disrupted two major Western pillars of globalization. Brexit has raised existential questions over the future prospects of deepening European Union integration. While Trump's presidency appears to have departed from the long-standing bipartisan tradition of American support for global liberalization. Trump's turn to protectionist tariffs against China and his threats against the EU, Canada, and Mexico have raised the threat of a global trade war. And Brexit's call to 'take back control' is an important symbolic reaction to the feeling that changes associated with globalization have eroded national sovereignty and disempowered communities. Deep fractures have opened up within the European Union, pitting creditor nations against debtors, and pro-immigration regimes and parties against their anti-immigration counterparts. New fault lines have emerged within Western politics. Further afield, the rise of authoritarian powers like China and the geopolitical resurgence of Putin's Russia have weakened the global grip of liberal democracy, severing the assumed link between economic globalization and political and social liberalism. As climate change gathers momentum, the challenges to retaining an open and integrated world market will grow.

Despite the severity of these challenges, this book argues that we are not witnessing the end of globalization. What we are seeing is the latest period of instability caused by a long-standing tension between ambitious liberal visions for how to organize an integrated world economy and the continued existence of sovereign nation states that respond to popular pressures to shelter their societies from the uneven impacts of globalized markets. As Chapter 2 shows, this tension has been a recurring theme of the longer history of globalization. It spans from the birth of the liberal political economy that has been the intellectual guide to globalization since the late eighteenth century, until today.

Different liberal doctrines of political economy have identified different ways to connect domestic economies to international flows of trade and capital. The more ambitiously market-fundamentalist of these visions, from the classical liberalism of the nineteenth century to the neoliberalism that has guided recent decades of globalization, have produced intensely uneven social and economic outcomes. This has helped to generate popular political projects that look to harness the power of the state to curb market excesses and reassert sovereignty. Projects that seek to restore the power and political vitality of the state are not doomed to be negative and destructive. They have the potential to be progressive – by rebuilding a genuine commitment to national and local democracy alongside a reassertion of inclusive social values, a thicker and more flexible conception of citizenship, and increased economic equality. But they can also be deeply regressive – strengthening the grip of authoritarian impulses that threaten democratic pluralism, denigrating 'outsider' groups, defending the interests of entrenched oligarchic economic elites by asphyxiating the structures of democratic accountability.

We are living through a period in which the darkly regressive dimension of these nation state restoration projects is in the ascendancy, from Donald Trump in the United States, to Jair Bolsonaro in Brazil, and Narendra Modi in India. These regressive nationalist efforts to steer the global market are on the rise as the popular legitimacy of globalization has been eroded by the inequalities and instability it has produced. But as Chapter 3 shows, this crisis is very different from that of the 1930s. We should not be paralysed by the fatalistic conclusion that we are inescapably doomed to repeat the failures of the past. The condition of globalization is now much deeper and broader than before. The structural interdependence of the world economy has increased, and the difficulties and costs associated with attempting to rapidly unravel interdependence have grown significantly. Modern politics, culture, and societies are different too, and while that clearly does not prevent the rise of political extremism it does mean that it will take different forms than those of the fascist militarism associated with the inter-war years. The crisis of the 1970s may hold more comparative clues for thinking historically about where we are today.

Rather than being the endpoint of globalization, Chapter 4 shows that the current travails of the world economy reflect a crisis of the more aggressively expansionist neoliberal era of globalization that emerged from the 1980s. A series of deep-rooted social and economic issues linked to the extension of globalization into ever-wider reaches of the world has interacted with more contingent geopolitical events to provoke the rise of xenophobic populism throughout much of the Western world. An ascendant and contradictory ideology of national liberalism has failed to provide progressive solutions to the economic problems associated with a world of increased trade and financial interdependence. Instead, it has shifted the blame for globalization's failures away from the wealthy architects and prime beneficiaries of our global economy and onto migrants, refugees, and other minority groups. To counter this trend, progressive forces need to revitalize the democratic project by tackling inequality, strengthening an active idea of citizenship, and decentralizing political and economic power wherever possible. This will involve less of certain kinds of global economic integration and more flexibility for governments to respond to the demands of their populations, but it should not mean the wholesale renunciation of globalization. It must also involve a renewed commitment to global solidarity and mutual aid, particularly as the challenge of climate change looms.

As the final chapter shows, the gravest challenge to the future of globalization may well come not from rising right-wing nationalism but from the effects of climate change. This has been the most important long-term legacy of the globalization project. Rapid ecological deterioration threatens the assumptions of unending growth, limitless energy use, and ever-increasing consumption that have shaped liberal understandings of how to organize our economics and politics. But the challenge of adjusting our economic and political systems to cope with climate change and halt its progress also represents a tremendous opportunity to create a different kind of globalization – one that retains a commitment to cosmopolitan values, interconnection, and interdependence, while curbing the worst excesses of our contemporary global economy and addressing the failure of international markets through a return to a more democratic and decentralized vision of economic planning and an enhanced commitment to global values of cross-border solidarity.

2

Globalization's four liberalisms

From its birth, globalization has been closely linked to liberal understandings of how to organize the economy. Liberal thinking about the relationship between politics and economics has guided the project of extending international trade and financial linkages around the world. But globalization has not been shaped by a singular intellectual vision. There has been significant variation between different liberal doctrines of political economy. At different moments, different liberal visions of how to organize the relationship between the domestic and international economy have been dominant. Some have called for a more unbridled endorsement of free trade and free movement of capital. Domestic goals and policy tools have been subordinated to the priorities of an open international economy. Other visions have been more circumspect, championing the benefits of free trade and cross-border capital flows, but recognizing the potential for international priorities to come into tension with domestic policies. Seeking to balance domestic policy priorities with the wider commitment to an interconnected global economy, they have prescribed

21

a significant role for states and international organizations in regulating trade and finance in the service of national democracy.

Four main liberal doctrines of political economy have guided globalization. Each vision has been associated with a gradual deepening of the globalized condition. But there has also been a gap between each different liberal vision of how to organize the global economy, understood as an ideal, and the practical workings of each era of globalization. This reflects an important truth – the liberal ideal is utopian. It can never be fully implemented in practice. It faces the enduring tension between the ideal of a globally interconnected world economy and the political division of the world into distinctive nation states, each with its own sovereign authority. Negotiating this tension has been an enduring challenge for the liberal architects of the globalization project. Unless the nation state is dissolved, something that seems extremely unlikely in a time of resurgent nationalism, this is a tension that cannot be overcome with any permanency.

As a result, the liberal project of globalization has to be reconfigured periodically as the temporary balance between domestic and international commitments, and between political–economic coalitions of social groups within and across states, unravels under economic and political strains. Economic and political crises emerge, reducing economic growth and weakening popular support for an open international economy. These crises have presented opportunities for alternative ideas and principles to shape the way in which the global economy is governed. Thinking in terms of the four guiding liberal visions of globalization can help us better situate the current crisis. This reveals that today's crisis of globalization is actually a more acute crisis of a distinctive 'neoliberal' vision of how to organize the global economy. The neoliberal vision has sought, since the late 1970s, to reassert the primacy of international trade and markets to the detriment of firmer control over domestic policy goals.

Separating politics and economics

Common to all liberal doctrines of political economy is a specific understanding of the relationship between politics and economics. Since the early nineteenth century, liberals have understood the 'economy' as a distinctive sphere of social life, one that is governed by its own laws. If politics is about the difficult task of resolving competing visions and priorities for governing society, economics is about the smooth interaction of individuals following their rational self-interest. Left to their own devices, these interests will generate an independent and self-sustaining order that benefits everyone. Within the free market, the adjustment of prices will bring the supply of and demand for goods into balance as individuals respond to changing incentives. This leads to harmonious and sustainable growth for the economy.

Not only is the economy distinct from politics, it is also the more foundational of the two spheres. The laws of the economy ground politics within certain parameters. Economic laws are not contingent or contestable in the way that political priorities and principles are. In this way, liberals enable the economy to set definite limits upon politics. Politics should not intrude destructively into the automatic mechanisms that govern the economic realm.[1] The market, as the embodiment of the economy, and the state, as the embodiment of politics, should remain separate and distinct. Private property, which ensures the strong feedback loop between individual effort and reward that motivates prosperity within capitalism, should not be challenged. Modern freedom can only be achieved if these boundaries are respected and protected.

Although the economy is distinct from politics, and the market distinct from the state, they are not entirely independent of each other. Liberals recognize that state institutions might need to intervene in the economy. But they disagree over the extent, frequency, and purpose of intervention. For some, the proper role of the state is simply to set in place the laws and dispense justice so that economic exchange can take place. In this view, states should ensure that contracts are respected, and private property rights upheld. For others, the state should play a more prominent role – providing those services and public goods that the market does not offer, and intervening to restore growth when the economy falls out of balance.

The practical recognition by liberals of the need for some state intervention within the economy highlights a fundamental weakness of the liberal vision – it is a convenient fiction. The economic and the political can never actually be separated in practice. Both are part of the wider social order. The forces that shape the interaction between the economy and the polity within capitalism, although distinctive, are constantly interacting and overlapping. Power relations are at work within both spheres. There are hierarchies and inequalities within

24

both, even when there are formal equalities under the law. Social inequalities of class, race, and gender shape both the political and the economic realms. The very dependence of private property upon the legal protection of the sovereign state testifies to the foundational and indissoluble links between politics and economics. These links are forged through the common currency of social power, which governs both realms. So, although liberals rightly recognize that the economy and politics became more distinctive (both institutionally and culturally) through the emergence of modern capitalism and are able to effectively highlight the benefits of this situation, they cannot fully evacuate politics and power from the economy.

There is also another purpose for which maintaining the fictional separation of politics and economics is necessary. It provides a solution to the following puzzle – how can we have an interconnected world economy governed by a natural order of economic laws within a political system of sovereign states? The notion that the economy and politics can be pulled apart is crucial for understanding how we can have economic interdependence without formal political subordination of one state to another. It is what distinguishes economic globalization from traditional imperialism. Liberal ideas about political economy help us understand how we can globalize our economies without giving up our national, territorial, political rights and prerogatives. Liberals promise us an interconnected global economy in which we can all share in the benefits of increased economic specialization and trade, without giving up our political sovereignty. This ability to deepen international economic connections while keeping political sovereignty should enable us to reconcile global capitalism and national democracy. Just as the idea of the separation of the economy and politics domestically is a fiction, though, so too is the idea that they can be fully separated internationally. In practice, globalization does involve important political and economic inequalities and patterns of hierarchy and domination. It has overlapped with and been brought about through forms of imperialism, colonialism, and neocolonialism.

Classical liberalism

The first wave of historical globalization was shaped by the ideas of classical liberalism. From the late eighteenth century, these ideas began to influence thinking about how to organize the domestic and international economy. At the heart of the classical liberal vision was an overarching faith in the free market and support for the expansion of free trade between nations. The free-market vision was most famously proposed by the Scottish political economist – Adam Smith. In *The Wealth of Nations*, published in 1776, Smith outlined his understanding of the invisible mechanisms that regulated the capitalist economy. Smith argued that the laws of the market would steer individual self-interest into a broader economic harmony. This could occur without recourse to government planning or pre-modern social customs. Competition between self-interested individuals would regulate economic interaction in a way that ensured that the goods produced were desired by society, were produced in the right quantities, and at a price society was willing to pay. Too much self-interest, in the form of the charging of extortionate prices, would price avaricious individuals out of the market. Given choice within a competitive market, consumers would simply refuse to pay such high prices. In this way, competition between producers within the market limited self-interest to a level that facilitated the wider harmony of the economy. In such a self-regulating market there was very minimal requirement for state intervention. This was the laissez-faire economy. It was regulated not by the benevolent foresight of the state, or the feudal bonds of custom, but by the 'invisible hand' – a hidden pattern of economic order generated by the unintended consequences of competitive interaction between self-interested individuals.[2]

Beneath the invisible hand of the market was a more readily identifiable structure. One that Smith saw as a major advantage of a capitalist market economy – the division of labour. By dividing up specific tasks within the factory, workers could enjoy major increases in productivity. Using the famous example of the pin factory, Smith suggested that the division of labour could enhance economic productivity in three ways. It could increase the 'dexterity' of each individual worker, improving their ability in their specialized task. It would also save time lost by switching from one task to another. And finally, it stimulated the development of labour-saving machines to perform simplified tasks.[3]

Smith's endorsement of the division of labour within England had important consequences for thinking about how to organize the international economy. The division of labour was limited in its scope by the size of the market. The larger the market, the higher the possibility for specialization and division among specific patterns of production, and therefore the greater the potential productivity of economic activity. Recognition of this led quite logically to the endorsement of free trade between nations and the rejection of protectionist impediments to international trade. Larger international markets would lead to greater production and greater wealth for those societies engaged. Free trade between nations could also enable the exchange of surplus domestic products for which there was no demand, for foreign goods in high demand.[4]

These early arguments for free trade were refined in the early nineteenth century by the English political economist, David Ricardo. Ricardo, a wealthy London businessman and man of letters, adopted a more abstract view of the economy than Smith. He further extended the idea of a separate economic realm with its own immutable laws. His theory of comparative advantage demonstrated formally how free trade could be beneficial to two trading partners, even if one of those countries was able to produce both goods more efficiently at home. A country need only have a comparative advantage (rather than an absolute advantage) in a particular area of production in order to benefit from free trade.

Using the example of trade between English cloth and Portuguese wine, Ricardo showed that even if Portugal could produce both cloth and wine more cheaply than England, thus having an absolute advantage in both, it would still make sense for the Portuguese to trade with the English. This was because importing cloth from England would allow Portugal to divert the freed-up capital and manpower away from cloth and toward the production of wine, in which Portugal could realize greater returns as her production of wine was more efficient than that of cloth. Similarly, for the English, the importation of Portuguese wine would free up capital and manpower for the production of cloth, in which England had a productive advantage when compared to the cost of producing wine domestically.[5]

How did these liberal ideas about trade shape patterns of early globalization? From the early nineteenth century, Britain, the industrial powerhouse of the world at that time, began to promote free trade. The most important development was the unilateral declaration of free trade in 1846 with the Repeal of the Corn Laws. These laws had controversially protected British farmers from foreign grain imports and were opposed by industrialists who wanted cheaper bread for their workforce. Declaring free trade unilaterally meant that there was no expectation that other countries would reciprocally reduce tariffs on corresponding products to access the British market. Britain moved steadily away from tariffs. Individual free trade advocates like Richard Cobden played an important role too, helping secure the important Cobden–Chevalier trade treaty of 1860 between Britain and France.

Free trade was adopted by various countries from the middle of the nineteenth century, but this was not simply a case of ascendant liberal ideas. The decision was often made more pragmatically as a way to secure access to Britain's large domestic market. In Germany, many industrialists continued to favour protectionism. While in France, free trade was also less popular than protectionism. But it was adopted nonetheless as part of a modernization strategy implemented by Emperor Napoleon III.[6] So, although the first wave of globalization is often viewed as the triumphant ascendance of liberal ideas about free trade, the basis of these ideas within the major European powers other than Britain was actually rather weak. Britain supported free trade so unequivocally because as the world's most competitive trading nation at the time, it benefited from a free trade order that allowed the importation of cheap food and other materials from abroad, freeing up Britain to focus on high value-added industrial goods.[7] And Britain had already reached a high level of industrialization before it adopted free trade, putting it in a strong competitive position to remove protection for its industries. A competitive advantage in international trade was a luxury unavailable to many later industrializing countries.[8]

Trade volumes did increase during the nineteenth century. International trade grew by 30 per cent between 1800 and 1830 and then increased fivefold between 1840 and 1870.[9] This growth in trade volumes was linked to the commitment to freer trade, but the motivations were often not a reflection of a wholesale conviction in classical liberal ideals. The nineteenth-century free trade order only ever had shallow roots, even within the dominant European economies. During the 1870s and 1880s, the major Western European states began to abandon free trade in favour of protectionism and the rising United States followed the same course.[10]

Outside of Europe the prevalence of free trade ideas was even more limited. Here, Britain's imperial domination of colonies played a much more important role in driving the development of a globally interconnected economy. In order to secure its early advantage in textiles, Britain prohibited the importation of printed calicoes from India. Britain also initially implemented high tariffs on Indian iron imports. And when free trade did arrive in India, it was a result of British imperial imposition.[11] Far from the separation of politics and economics, then, the classical liberal order involved the fusion of the two through the coercive imposition of free trade within Britain's colonized and racially subordinated imperial supply zones. Imperialism and free trade went hand in hand.

Unequal trade treaties were imposed on a range of countries, from Brazil to China, Japan, and the Ottoman Empire. They were part of a wider 'civilizing mission' adopted by Britain and other European powers who viewed non-Europeans and non-Christians as racially inferior. Whereas European trade treaties were negotiated in a contractual approach, throughout the non-European world free trade was imposed, often through the threat of British naval incursion.[12] The maintenance of rival imperial economic zones administered by the European great powers set limits on the scope of a universal market and proved an obstacle to a deeper and more consensual basis for globalization.

Nineteenth-century globalization was not just about trade, however. It also involved an unprecedented degree of financial integration. In order to transact the growing volume of trade, countries needed a common international payments system. This came in the shape of the classical gold standard. Under the gold standard, individual countries fixed their exchange rates to one another by promising that their domestic currency could be presented on demand for exchange into a legally defined quantity of gold. The system fostered increased trade by ensuring that currency values were stable, reducing the risk that changes in exchange rates

31

might jeopardize the profitability of transactions. It also encouraged a growing volume of capital flows across borders for investment purposes. From the early 1870s, more and more countries moved onto the gold standard.

Just as trade dynamics had been influenced by liberal ideas, so too was the gold standard. The mechanics of the system were laid out most explicitly by David Hume in his 'price-specie flow model'. According to this model, the gold standard would work automatically to balance trade flows between countries over time. If a country exported more than it imported, running a trade surplus, gold from abroad would flow into the economy in payment for the exported goods. This would increase the domestic gold supply and, because the level of domestic money was linked to the supply of metallic gold that could be coined at the mint, it would lead to rising prices (with more money now chasing the same amount of goods). In this way, the trade surplus country's exports would become more expensive for foreigners and the volume of exports would decrease. The higher prices and domestic money supply would have the opposite effect on imports – making them cheaper and increasing their volume. For the country with the trade deficit (importing more than it exported), the gold outflows to the surplus country would reduce the domestic gold supply and lead to lower prices. This would make the deficit country's exports cheaper and more competitive, while making imports from abroad more expensive. This would rebalance the trade position between the two countries.[13]

Mirroring the gap between theory and reality seen with trade, though, the practices of the gold standard deviated widely from their mechanistic representation in liberal writing. Rather than the 'automatic' adjustment that was supposed to occur through the movement of gold, the central banks of major economies like France, Germany, and Britain actually intervened, setting interest rates to influence the domestic money supply and prevent gold outflows. Most payments were actually settled not with gold but with credit based on Britain's pound sterling.[14] In reality, this was a system tightly configured around Britain's imperial power but relying on the actions of other powerful countries who adopted the gold standard in line with their own national interests. Within the British colonies, the need for a reliable supply of gold from countries like South Africa and India was linked not to liberal governance but to the imposition of tighter colonial control.[15]

Although the ideas of classical liberalism did influence the first wave of globalization, they were never implemented in line with the expectations of theory. Instead they were grafted unevenly onto a world economy in which imperial domination of the non-European economies continued to play a crucial role and modernizing elites often sought protectionist remedies and nationalist strategies to harness the benefits of industrialization. This first wave of globalization significantly enhanced economic interdependence by increasing trade and financial flows alongside the mass movement of populations. Technologically, innovations like the telegraph and the steam ship helped to compress space and time, speeding up the ability to connect different economies around the world.[16] But the nascent globalized condition linked to increases in flows of trade, money, and people was characterized by its fragility. It unravelled spectacularly under the pressure of two world wars and the Great Depression between 1914 and 1945.

Embedded liberalism

The classical liberal era of globalization came to an end with the outbreak of the First World War in 1914. It had always contained within it powerful elements of nationalism, protectionism, and imperialism that jarred with the universalist principles of liberal doctrine. These elements had become more pronounced in the years before the war. After the war ended the major powers attempted to remake the old liberal system of trade and finance. But under the radically altered conditions that followed from the First World War, and the strains of the Great Depression, the project failed. The restored gold standard lasted only from 1925 to 1931, and by the early 1930s, major powers like Britain and the United States had gone off gold and implemented trade protectionism. Britain turned to its protected imperial markets. Communist revolution transformed Russia's politics and economics after 1917. While in Germany, Japan, and Italy, fascism and the shift to a war economy took hold. Despite Woodrow Wilson's pronouncement of a new liberal vision for world politics at Versailles in 1919, the colonized and imperially subjugated countries remained subject to a racialized exclusion from the liberal principles applied to the great powers.[17]

It was not until after the Second World War that a successful attempt at relaunching the liberal vision of globalization occurred. The Bretton Woods Agreement of 1944, which brought together leaders from around the world to develop blueprints for the post-war international trade and financial system, heralded the launch of the 'embedded liberal' vision of globalization. This embedded liberal vision departed from classical liberalism in several important ways. It looked to preserve the classical liberal commitment to an open international economy based on increased free trade and a stable international payments system. But it recognized that the classical liberal vision for the international economy needed to be balanced with important domestic policy goals. Achieving this balance would require the imposition of selective restrictions on the mobility of capital and the freedom of trade. These restrictions were seen as essential to achieving the newly accepted goals of social welfare and full employment that had not been properly protected by the design of the nineteenth-century international economy.[18]

The most important intellectual figure in guiding the new embedded liberal vision was the British economist, John Maynard Keynes. Keynes developed many of his most influential economic ideas in works published during the turbulent inter-war years of the 1920s and 1930s. He occupied a unique position within British society, straddling his academic role as a Cambridge don alongside his duties as a civil servant and adviser to the UK government, while also being a prominent member of the avant-garde Bloomsbury set of artists and intellectuals. His thinking about political economy was very much a product of his age. It was a response to the major challenges of the times – the rebuilding of the international economy after the First World War and the Great Depression of the 1930s.

Keynes had been critical of the terms imposed on

the defeated powers at Versailles in 1919, arguing that the onerous debt burden would prevent swift economic recovery during the 1920s. He was also opposed to the restoration of the gold standard after the war. Keynes was keen to avoid the impact of the gold standard in shaping the domestic money supply. One of the effects of the gold standard had been a deflationary bias – the gold basis of the money supply set a limit on the capacity for its expansion and limited economic growth. Additionally, without the ability to adjust exchange rates, the pressure of adjustment to trade deficits led to the reduction of domestic prices and government spending through austerity. This undermined the potential for full employment and, since wages were the most flexible and significant component of prices, led to declining incomes for workers. Keynes argued instead that the money supply should be geared towards achieving full employment, with the exchange rate adjusting to reflect this.[19]

More influential than his views on the gold standard, though, was Keynes' vision for the management of the domestic economy as a whole. In October 1929 the value of securities on the New York Stock Exchange collapsed during the Wall Street Crash. Massive bank failures and huge unemployment followed as the American economy ground to a halt and the international financial system came under huge strain. Grappling with the Depression that followed from the crash, Keynes developed new ideas about how to maintain stable growth within a capitalist economy. In his 1936 *General Theory of Employment, Interest and Money*, Keynes challenged the classical liberal faith in the capacity of the economy to achieve sustained growth through the natural equilibrium between supply and demand. Keynes argued that capitalist economies might not always achieve balance. Instead they could remain trapped in a long-term state of depressed growth, falling income, and declining employment.[20]

With business confidence diminished during a downturn, the level of idle savings would increase relative to productive investment in the economy. The decline in investment would reduce the level of demand in the economy and further check its expansion due to falling prices and rising unemployment. Over the long term this imbalance between savings and investment wouldn't lead to ever-increasing levels of savings. In fact, falling incomes due to recession would lead to decreasing savings. The economy would be left gridlocked and inert. Responding to this condition, Keynes suggested that governments needed to step in, providing spending and investment to boost demand in the economy and restore growth.[21] Keynes envisaged a more activist role for government, adjusting the level of spending and taxation to achieve a volume of overall economic output that would enable full employment. This would involve the use of public investment, in infrastructure or other public works programmes, to supplement private investment during a downturn.[22] During boom periods, governments would raise taxes and/or curb spending to cool the potential for an overheating economy. The state would have a much more prominent role in overseeing the economy and managing the fluctuations of the business cycle.

Keynes' role as a civil servant within the UK Treasury during the inter-war years gave his ideas a unique proximity to the practical management of the economy. But despite this access, it was only during the 1940s that Keynes' ideas really began to gain traction in reshaping official economic policy in Britain. His ideas were part of a wider shift in liberal economic thinking that had important parallels in the United States. After the failure of the initial classical laissez-faire response to the Depression, American economists such as Alvin Hansen challenged the classical view. They called for greater government influence in setting prices and managing economic growth so as to achieve a more stable level of employment.[23] Under President Roosevelt's second administration, from 1937, these ideas began to gain ground.[24] Young university graduates, inspired by Keynes' *General Theory*, were steadily recruited into government agencies responsible for managing economic policy.[25] New Deal investment programmes and the mobilization of the war economy put these ideas into practice.

The rise of new economic thinking in Britain and the United States had a major influence on the Anglo-American blueprint for relaunching economic globalization put in place at Bretton Woods. To achieve balance between the international priorities of free trade and monetary stability, on the one hand, and domestic goals of welfare provision, stable growth and full employment, on the other, a new set of international institutions was designed. Keynes personally represented Britain in the negotiations at Bretton Woods, while Harry Dexter White led the American team. Keynes and Dexter White disagreed on a number of issues, reflecting the sharply different interests of the two countries, with Britain crippled by massive war debts and American power greatly augmented by the end of the war. But they agreed on two key principles that would shape the post-war globalization project. Firstly, that the movement of international capital could not be allowed to undermine the policy flexibility for national governments looking to promote social welfare and full employment. And secondly, that fully liberalized capital flows were not compatible with the exchange rate stability required to promote the recovery of international trade. It must therefore be permissible for governments to regulate the flow of capital across borders in the services of their national economic and social goals. Keynes and White had learnt the lessons of the inter-war years, where short-term speculative capital movements between countries had led to exchange rate instability, domestic economic malaise, and declining trade.[26]

This consensus on the need to curb the freedom of international capital movements was embodied in the new institutions and principles set down at Bretton Woods. Exchange rates would be fixed as they had been during the heyday of nineteenth-century globalization, in order to create a conducive environment for increased international trade. But they would now be adjustable so that countries had more flexibility to respond to trade imbalances without sacrificing domestic welfare and employment through the need for deflationary austerity policies. Capital flows would now be restricted by legal controls on cross-border currency movements in an attempt to protect domestic governments from the pressures of speculative capital flight and currency instability. And two new institutions, the International Monetary Fund (IMF) and the International Bank for Reconstruction and Development (subsequently known as the World Bank), were established to manage different aspects of international finance. The IMF would monitor national economic policies and provide emergency funding to assist countries that were struggling to manage trade imbalances. The International Bank for Reconstruction and Development would provide long-term finance to assist investment projects in countries looking to rebuild their economies after the devastation of the war. The US dollar, reflecting the unparalleled economic strength of the United States, would act as the key international currency, convertible to gold on demand at the fixed price of $35 per ounce.[27]

With regard to international trade, the General Agreement on Tariffs and Trade (GATT) was established shortly after Bretton Woods. This new multilateral agreement between 23 countries, which steadily expanded its membership in the years that followed, would help advance the goal of enhancing free trade by overseeing a gradual reduction of tariffs. GATT was governed by three key principles that embedded free trade within a deeper international regime. It promoted non-discrimination, multilateral approaches to dealing with trade, and the application of the Most Favoured Nation principle (by which a favour granted to one trading partner must be extended to all). Trade was to be expanded through the progressive reduction of barriers. And all signatories to the agreement were committed to unconditional reciprocity in their trading relations with one another.

The new framework established at Bretton Woods gave the globalization project a much deeper institutional grounding than it had experienced during the nineteenth century. Global economic integration gradually increased, and the early post-war decades witnessed an unprecedented period of sustained economic growth within the international economy.[28] The creation of a stable international payments system allowed rapid growth in world trade. The total volume of merchandise exports from non-communist countries grew by 290 per cent between 1948 and 1968.[29] The rules-based nature of the new system gave it greater legitimacy, and a deeper and wider basis of support than the nineteenth-century globalization project that had pivoted around British imperial power. Now it was the United States' hegemonic power that stood at the heart of the system. Bretton Woods managed to balance gradual economic integration and rapid growth with a high level of domestic welfare, avoiding the worst economic excesses of the 1920s and 1930s, maintaining higher welfare spending alongside rising living standards in the Western economies. And in a post-war era that began to see widespread decolonization as national independence movements broke free from the shackles of empire, the Bretton Woods agreement provided an early vision for the development of poorer countries in the Global South. This foreshadowed the way in which the post-war approach to what were now termed 'developing' countries would depart substantially from the imperial domination characteristic of nineteenth-century globalization.[30]

Despite these achievements, though, the embedded liberal era failed to find a sustainable balance between international liberal commitments and the domestic policy priorities of individual nation states. When push came to shove, the dollar's role at the heart of the renewed international payments system was undermined by America's desire to prioritize national interests and economic autonomy above the sacrifices required to ensure the stability of the wider monetary system.[31] By 1971, the United States had ended the dollar's link to gold and terminated the Bretton Woods monetary system of fixed exchange rates. Protectionist interests also regained momentum in the United States as the increased competitiveness of European and Japanese producers eroded American trade dominance.[32] Despite the early promise of the GATT, most signatories other than the United States had only achieved minimal tariff reductions before the late 1960s.[33] In terms of its restrictions on the movement of private capital flows, Bretton Woods did enable a balance between national economic development and increased international trade at first. But the efficacy of the controls rapidly declined during the 1960s, as the development of offshore financial markets in the City of London and the use of accounting devices enabled national capital controls to be circumvented with increasing ease. This generated mounting pressure on the system of fixed exchange rates, as growing volumes of speculative money could wreak havoc on national currencies.

In the arena of support for developing countries, the early Bretton Woods enthusiasm for provision of public development finance and policy space was abandoned as the interests of private financiers achieved renewed prominence under President Truman's administration and the development of the Cold War antagonism shifted US strategic priorities. State-led development strategies now appeared, through the polarizing Cold War ideological lens of 'free markets vs socialist planning', as erring too far from the former and too close to the latter.[34] The existence of a separate Soviet sphere of economic influence, closed off to Western trade and capital flows, set an important geographical limit upon the reach of post-war globalization. Cold War rivalry ensured that embedded liberal ideas were contested by socialist and communist alternatives that held the reach of Western pro-market influence in check and limited the breadth of the globalized condition that was slowly intensified in the decades after Bretton Woods.

Neoliberalism

The embedded liberal phase of globalization came unstuck during a decade of economic and political crisis in the 1970s. Changing domestic and international conditions disturbed the arrangements put in place at Bretton Woods. Political pressures within the Western political economies had risen during the 1960s. This culminated with widespread international protests throughout the summer of 1968, leading to major civil disturbance in the United States and the near-toppling of the government in France. Democracy was under strain. The political and economic settlement between business and workers put in place after the Second World War, which had been based on the suspension of the political conflict of the fractious inter-war years in favour of a shared commitment to enhancing economic growth and rising living standards, unravelled.[35]

Slowing economic growth, rising inflation, and increasing unemployment began to return distributional struggles to the heart of Western politics. Growing labour militancy and increasing wage demands generated inflationary pressures. The collapse of the Bretton Woods monetary system from 1971 led to heightened international financial instability. With fixed exchange rates abandoned by many countries, an important constraint on the domestic money supply was removed and inflation resulted as wage increases were accommodated. Financial deregulation began to ease the supply of credit, adding fuel to the inflationary fire. And in 1973 and 1974, major oil price increases by the newly formed OPEC oil cartel in the Middle East sent inflationary shockwaves through the world economy and provoked the onset of recession. Stagflation, the combination of high inflation and slow economic growth, entered the economic lexicon. Developing countries suffered as a result. Western economic slowdown led to a sharp decline in international demand for their exports. And as the cost of oil imports increased so too did the developing country debt burden. Having witnessed the limited success of their post-independence economic strategies, developing countries began to push for a transformation of the global economy through their vision for a 'New International Economic Order'.[36]

It was within this context of widespread international turmoil that the neoliberal challenge emerged. Just as embedded liberalism had sought to modify the premises of its classical liberal forebear, so too did neoliberal thinkers seek to displace and unsettle the ideas associated with embedded liberalism. They questioned the integrity of post-war 'liberal' values and took aim at the Keynesian-inspired economic ideas that had prevailed in the post-war period. Neoliberalism sought to restore a classical vision of liberalism in which the aspects of planning, welfarism, and economic management characteristic of post-war society would be scaled back, and the reign of market forces restored. But they departed from the classical vision in their view of the state. Rather than restoring the classical 'night-watchman' state of the nineteenth century, limited to the provision of security and the defence of property, neoliberals sought a more virile and positive state. One that would go beyond laissez-faire to actively promote and reproduce a competitive market order.[37]

Neoliberal ideas were incubated over a period of decades within a shadowy transnational group of fringe intellectuals. The term 'neoliberal' was coined at the 1938 Colloque Walter Lippmann in Paris. It referred to a belief in the importance of free enterprise, a competitive market order, and a state that was both powerful and impartial. The Paris meeting included fifteen figures who would go on to participate in the more infamous Mont Pelerin Society founded in 1947, which became the main forum for neoliberal discussion in the years ahead. The Mont Pelerin Society brought together figures from academia, media, politics, and business.[38] It included two individuals who would be particularly influential in driving the neoliberal challenge to post-war policy – the Austrian philosopher and economist Friedrich von Hayek, and the American economist Milton Friedman.

Hayek was the dominant intellectual figure associated with the neoliberal movement. He was the founding president of the Mont Pelerin Society. From his academic posts, first at the LSE and then the University of Chicago, Hayek attacked what he understood as the decay of Western liberalism and democracy. In his famous polemic, *The Road to Serfdom*, he argued that socialism, planning, and the veneration of expanded state provision of economic goods in the West were steps on a journey that would lead inevitably towards totalitarianism and repression.[39] As an alternative to this fate, Hayek looked to restore a society governed by the impersonal forces of the market. He referred to this as the 'catallaxy' – an order that would emerge spontaneously through the market as people followed their natural inclinations under the rule of law. Under this order, skill and chance would determine an individual's place in society. Much like Adam Smith before him, Hayek saw government interference in the production, distribution, and pricing of goods as damaging to the natural order of the market. Such interference against the market could only ever be unjust, distorting the allocation of rewards and arbitrarily privileging favoured groups.[40]

The ideas of Hayek and other neoliberal thinkers remained marginal during the early post-war decades. But as the crisis of post-war Keynesianism intensified from the late 1960s, their efforts to keep an alternative political and economic vision alive began to bear fruit. One of the major beneficiaries of greater public receptiveness to these ideas was Milton Friedman. Friedman was a professor at the University of Chicago, where Hayek had moved after the Second World War to establish an American stronghold for his project of renewing liberalism. Closely linked to the Mont Pelerin Society in origin, the 'Chicago Schools' of law and economics proselytized neoliberal ideas within the academy.[41] Friedman came to be a leading economist within the economics faculty. His 1962 work *Capitalism and Freedom* sought to mask the role of corporate power in contemporary society by directing criticism towards government for the introduction of monopolies that distorted the market.[42]

Friedman's most notable contribution, though, came in the more arcane world of monetary theory. As runaway inflation and economic stagnation became the dominant economic policy concerns from the late 1960s, Friedman set to work unpicking the central tenets of Keynesian-inspired approaches to managing the economy. It was through this avenue that neoliberal ideas first began to influence mainstream political discourse. Friedman's disagreement with Keynes hinged on the centrality and efficacy of interest rates to shaping dynamics within the economy. Friedman argued that Keynes had underestimated the importance of a stable money supply to steady economic growth. The turn to fiscal policy as a way to manage the level of aggregate demand in the economy under Keynesianism had neglected the importance of monetary policy.[43] Operating with a revived 'quantity theory of money', through which inflation and the excessive expansion of the money supply were understood to be synonymous, Friedman called for greater focus on monetary dynamics.[44] But he also challenged the technical basis of monetary policy, arguing that interest rates were an unreliable indicator, due to the lagged nature of their effects on inflation. Instead attention should be paid to regulating the quantity of money itself through setting target levels of money circulating within the economy.[45]

Additionally, Friedman and like-minded economists attacked Keynesian-inspired ideas that had shaped understanding of the relationship between unemployment and inflation. Under the prevailing 'Phillips Curve' it was understood that there was a negative relationship between unemployment and inflation – if unemployment increased then inflation decreased and vice versa. This posed policy-makers with a choice to make; either aim for full employment and expect higher inflation. Or accept some unemployment to avoid increasing inflation. Friedman cast doubt on this theory, suggesting that in the longer term it was hard for policy-makers to balance the two objectives. He argued instead that underlying structural factors within the economy led to a 'natural' rate of unemployment. Policy-makers could only keep unemployment above or below that natural rate in the short term, by distorting the level of inflation in the economy with damaging effects.[46] Friedman also attacked the role of capital controls and fixed exchange rates, preferring the free operation of market forces in the international financial system.[47]

These ideas began to gain influence among policy and political elites within the West after having first been tested out on the crisis-stricken Chilean economy after the 1973 coup d'état by General Augusto Pinochet. They were taken up most vigorously in Britain and the United States, the main architects of the post-war international economic order. Both Thatcher and Reagan embarked on policy programmes of far-reaching financial deregulation, empowering the financial sector in the process. They also sought to tackle head-on the vested interests that they viewed as obstacles to the free operation of the market. Confrontations with the trade union movements in both countries reset the balance of power between business and workers and tore up the more conciliatory pattern of labour relations set in place after the Second World War. Friedman's monetarist theory was applied to central bank policy with (at best) mixed results, but the imposition of high interest rates helped provoke economic recession and higher unemployment, gradually squeezing inflation out of the economy. The economic impasse of the 1970s was redressed in favour of a strong reassertion of business power and the rule of the market. By the 1990s, parties on both the left and the right throughout the world had begun to reshape their policies in line with some of the core principles of neoliberalism.

Internationally, neoliberal ideas began to reshape the role of the Bretton Woods institutions under the auspices of America's global dominance. The emergence of the 'Washington Consensus' around free-market policies during the 1980s and 1990s led to a more aggressively pro-market stance within the IMF, World Bank, and World Trade Organization. These changes tipped the balance towards a stronger promotion of free trade and free capital flows and away from the protection of domestic commitments to welfare and full employment enshrined after the Second World War. In developing countries, the IMF and World Bank pursued Structural Adjustment Programmes, using the increased indebtedness of poorer countries that had been intensified by high interest rates in Britain and the United States (home to the major banks lending the money) during the 1980s to leverage opening of their markets, privatization, tough anti-inflationary policies and dismantling of the public sector as a quid pro quo for assistance with debt repayment. Across sub-Saharan Africa these policies had devastating effects.[48] The United States now pressed the free trade agenda more aggressively through the WTO. Formed in 1995, the WTO was a more formalized and binding version of GATT, with a broader mandate and mechanisms for settling trade disputes and enforcing trade rules.[49] The WTO liberalization agenda encroached into markets that had been protected after the Second World War in the interests of ensuring high domestic employment and economic stability. The average tariff on manufactured goods had fallen from 40 per cent in 1947 to around five per cent by 2009.[50] There were 153 member countries of the WTO by 2008, accounting for nearly 100 per cent of world trade.

The rise to prominence of neoliberal ideas both reflected and reinforced the increased power of global corporations and global finance. As the power of finance and Multinational Corporations (MNCs) increased there was a corresponding weakening of the trade unions and socialist parties that had previously counterbalanced their influence. Multinationals used offshoring strategies to escape higher labour costs in the West and developed vast global production networks to take advantage of cheaper labour, looser regulation, and tax incentives in other countries. This had the effect of deepening and widening the international division of labour, with more parts of the world economy integrated into the expanding web of global production. To give an example, the clothing company Nike runs a manufacturing network that involves over 700 factories across 42 different countries.[51] China's gradual entry into the world market from the late 1970s was a game-changer in this regard. And when China joined the WTO in 2001, hundreds of millions of cheap labourers were brought into the globalized economy. By the 2000s, MNCs accounted for around 50 per cent of world trade.[52]

With the restrictions on capital mobility put in place at Bretton Woods gradually overturned, global capital flows increased enormously during the neoliberal era. Throughout the 1980s, Foreign Direct Investment increased by 14 per cent annually, while during the 1990s that figure rose to 20 per cent.[53] Short-term capital flows, often highly speculative in nature, also rose spectacularly. The average volume of foreign exchange dealings (in which national currencies are traded) rose from $15 billion per day in 1973 to $5.3 trillion in 2013. By the early 2000s, it took foreign exchange markets just one day to trade the value of annual world GDP.[54]

Rapid growth in trade and financial flows led to a profound intensification of the globalized condition during the neoliberal era. The international division of labour was broadened and deepened, bringing in massive emerging markets like China and India, while integrating more sectors of each national economy into globalized trade and production networks. This process was aided by important breakthroughs in information technology from the 1980s. The development of the internet and fibre optic cables sped up global communications, helping to shrink time and space. Geopolitically, the collapse of the Soviet Union expanded the reach of the globalization project into the former Soviet economies. The neoliberal project relied on the implementation of binding rules that were created through institutions geared towards protecting markets from intervention by democratic forces.[55] This led to a more constitutionalized basis for globalization that shrank the space for national policy choices – from European integration to the more formalized and binding rules of the WTO.[56]

As we shall see in Chapter 4, though, although neoliberalism was associated with a major deepening and widening of the globalized condition, it also undermined support for globalization by removing the commitment to domestic employment and social welfare associated with the embedded liberal era. In freeing financial markets from their post-war constraints and weakening the power of workers, neoliberalism sowed the seeds for spiralling inequality alongside a series of financial crises that culminated spectacularly in 2007/8. And as the rules-based regional integration projects that drove neoliberal globalization intensified, from NAFTA to the EU, they threatened national political sovereignty and transformed societies in ways that prompted a popular political backlash.

National liberalism

Neoliberalism's dominance was finally disrupted by the Global Financial Crisis of 2007/8. But although the neoliberal order has been gravely weakened, with populist politics reshaping Western liberal democracies, it has not been displaced. No coherent ideological alternative has emerged. Nor does there appear to be a clearly formed alternative liberal vision waiting in the wings. Instead, we have witnessed a resurgent right-wing nationalism and increasing xenophobia grafted onto the continued defence of the free market. The character of this transformation is not the same in all countries. But the theme of rising nationalist sentiment and dissatisfaction with globalization is a common theme. This emergent 'national liberalism' has been embodied by the Anglo-American political revolts of Britain's vote for Brexit and the United States' election of President Donald Trump. Embracing xenophobia, and the castigation of targeted minorities, national liberalism represents a new and dangerous phase of globalization. One in which the tolerance and pluralism of social liberalism is in peril of being abandoned, while the distributional and ecological catastrophes of neoliberalism remain unchallenged by incumbent elites. In parts of Central and Eastern Europe, these dynamics are generating even more intensely xenophobic and socially illiberal politics. In the latest phase of globalization, the tension between the sovereign state and global markets is crystallizing around the politics of migration because of the ascendancy of right-wing political tendencies.

The rise of extreme right-wing nationalist politics today is a reminder that the liberal visions of political economy that have guided globalization have the tendency to produce powerful social and political reactions. The attempt to separate politics and economics, while combining international economic integration with formal political sovereignty, is a false promise. The uneven distribution of costs and benefits associated with globalization, and the threat to political sovereignty posed by deeper forms of international economic integration, can provoke politically toxic attempts to protect the nation state from the forces of the world economy. International economic and political crises have punctuated the longer history of globalization, unsettling the temporary balance between domestic and international priorities shaped by different liberal ideas about political economy. National liberalism, as Chapter 4 shows, is a dangerous tendency that threatens to undo the positive values of social liberalism without tackling the deep structural problems within contemporary globalization. But the question that remains to be answered is just how dangerous the threat posed by national liberalism is? And whether the end-game for the liberal visions of globalization will be the turn, once more, to the fascism and militarism of the 1930s?

3

Why we are not in the 1930s

The shadow of the 1930s looms large over contemporary politics. Resurgent right-wing nationalism and the rise of populist leaders, from Washington DC to Ankara and Delhi, have stirred troubling memories of Hitler and Mussolini. The slowdown in economic growth and stalled living standards since the financial crisis carry echoes of the Great Depression. Fears abound that deep economic malaise will provide a fertile soil within which the twisted roots of fascism can grow. Liberal cosmopolitan values appear to be in full retreat under the pressures of xenophobia, protectionism, great power politics, and the reassertion of national sovereignty. The refrain that we are moving into a dark era of barbarity akin to the 1930s is now a commonplace.

Do the deep fissures within the politics of contemporary globalization really bear much resemblance to the singularly catastrophic decade of the 1930s? A decade that brought the world to ruin through spectacular industrial violence and trawled the darkest depths of inhumanity. Are we likely to see a repeat disintegration of the global economy into rival exclusive blocs of protected trade and tightly controlled national finance? Although the historical analogy of the 1930s is a tempting way to make sense of what is happening today it is also deeply misleading. Globalization is in crisis. But when we look more carefully the characteristics of this crisis are very different to the challenges faced in the 1930s.

We now live in a much more pervasive condition of globalization. Interdependence is broader and deeper than ever before. This means that today's crisis of globalization bears closer resemblance to another, more recent, period of turbulence for the politics of global economic integration. If we are to draw any illuminating historical parallel to make sense of the politics of today it is to the crisis of the 1970s that we should look. Despite the prevalence of the 1930s as the historical reference point for much of the alarm over the breakdown of globalization, the crisis of the 1970s is actually more helpful for understanding contemporary problems. That is because, as we saw in the previous chapter, globalization is of a qualitatively different form and magnitude today. There are hugely important differences within the international economic and political system of today when compared to the 1930s. The context of rival imperialisms within the West, a hallmark of the period between the 1870s and 1940s, has been surpassed. War itself has also changed dramatically. In the nuclear age of 'Mutually Assured Destruction' conflict on a scale equivalent to that which previously disrupted the global market order during the twentieth century is unlikely. And when it comes to economic relations, the patterns of global production and vast international capital flows that characterize today's global economy massively raise the costs of disintegration, limiting the potential for autarky.

Much in the same way that the crisis of the 1970s did not lead to the wholesale disintegration of the globalization project, as many had feared at the time, so too is today's crisis unlikely to undo interdependence completely – at least in the short to medium term. Instead, the Brexit vote and the election of Donald Trump represent an attempt to renegotiate selectively the *terms and conditions* of globalization, rather than an attempt to move towards wholesale deglobalization. Even if globalization as *process* has stalled, globalization as *condition* will be very hard to unwind, given the profound levels of structural economic interdependence within contemporary global capitalism. The enormous political difficulties surrounding Brexit demonstrate just how challenging it is to disentangle from the deepest forms of economic and political integration associated with globalization.

This should not, though, be read as a claim that we are not in a dangerous moment. Politics does not always follow the parameters of reason. Fear and emotion are hugely important too. Because the globalized condition is so much more pervasive today the disruption caused by its unravelling, should that occur, will be much greater. And the politics that flows from the breakdown of globalization may perhaps prove even darker. Deeper globalization makes it harder to reject interdependence and turn to autarky. But it also makes such a transition, should the political determination to push it through emerge, potentially more damaging.

The temptation to view the turmoil afflicting contemporary global politics through the mirror image of the

1930s stems from a number of similarities. Then, just as now, xenophobic nationalism was on the rise. Fascist political parties turned to the racialized denigration of 'outsiders' to create their exclusionary vision of the nation. Using the firebrand rhetoric that we associate with today's populist leaders like Trump and Erdogan, demagogues like Mussolini and Hitler used extreme oratory to subvert democracy and stir popular passions. And in the 1930s, much as today, the fallout from a severe economic crisis plagued politics. In an era of economic depression distributional struggles intensified, workers were pitted against bosses, and nationalistic rivalry between states was used to deflect criticism away from the failures of capitalism. The parallels go further. The 1930s represented the final anguished passing of Britain's leadership of the international economy and the rise of contender powers from Germany, to Japan, and the (eventually dominant) United States. We might reasonably view today's post-crisis global economy as marked by a similar pattern of fractious great power transition, with the United States in terminal decline and a rapidly rising China soon to take up the mantle of international dominance.

Tempting as it may be, thinking in these terms actually leaves us floundering within a shallow and superficial historical comparison. If we dig a little deeper, it soon becomes clear that the differences between then and now are much greater than the similarities. The 1930s was a unique period in the history of the international economy. The intensity of the economic breakdown and political rivalry that marked the inter-war years was the product of factors specific to that time. And although there are common tensions between globalizing markets and sovereign states that can be seen both then and now, the challenge of the 1930s was much graver. As we saw in the previous chapter, the classical liberal age of globalization began to disintegrate from the late nineteenth century. The severity of the breakdown of this first incarnation of the globalization project was a consequence of both the comparatively shallow roots of early globalization, when compared to today, and the combination of the effects of the First World War and the fallout from the Great Depression. Both of these shocks were much more severe than anything we have experienced in recent years and they occurred within a context of a less intensely globalized and more fragile international economy. Understanding the big differences between then and now can help us locate more clearly how to think about the politics of globalization.

The problems of the inter-war economy

To understand the cataclysm of the 1930s we need to cast our gaze back to the First World War and the collapse of the classical liberal order. The rise of fascism and the breakdown of the first wave of economic globalization were part of what the English historian E. H. Carr referred to as the 'twenty years crisis' – a period of deep economic and political instability that spanned from 1919 to 1939.[1] Bookending this period were the two world wars. Intertwined political and economic crises leading up to 1939 reflected the failure to effectively rebuild a liberal international economic order after the First World War.

One of the major problems here was the attempt to

restore the gold standard payments system during the 1920s. Britain had stood at the centre of the pre-war gold standard. But the war accelerated a pattern of relative economic decline underway since the late nineteenth century. Britain's share of world trade had fallen from 30 per cent in the mid nineteenth century to just 14.1 per cent by 1913. Germany and the United States, Britain's major economic and political competitors, had seen corresponding increases in their shares. Britain also began to lose its leading edge in critical areas of industrial production, falling behind in the Second Industrial Revolution centred on innovations in chemicals, electricity, steel, and transportation. Germany and the United States dominated in these cutting-edge areas while also pioneering industrial management strategies that outdid Britain.[2] The war only deepened Britain's economic decline despite the fact that Germany was also gravely weakened. Foreign markets were lost to competitors and huge borrowing from the United States to fund the war effort turned Britain from a creditor to a debtor. Debt servicing would consume a huge 40 per cent of Britain's budget during the 1920s.[3] These changes meant that the restoration of an international economic order with Britain at its heart would be based on much weaker foundations than before. British credit and lending from London would not be able to underwrite world economic growth as it previously had.

Added to the weakening of Britain's role as the financial and trading pivot around which economic globalization turned was a wider disruption of the international economy. High levels of inflation caused by war-time spending disrupted the exchange rates that had prevailed before the war and undermined the potential for stable trading patterns. Rising prices led to the erosion of the real value of workers' wages and sparked a growing wave of trade union militancy and class conflict.[4] These were the deeply inauspicious conditions within which the restoration of the gold standard was attempted. Applying the old gold standard logic, governments attempted to squeeze down wages and make their exports more competitive to improve their trade balance by restoring their pre-war currency values. But the effect was to provoke increased resistance from workers. With more workers now unionized and backed by emerging socialist parties, it was harder to bring about the adjustment in domestic prices that the gold standard relied on. Italian austerity fuelled the flames of fascism. While in Britain, the Labour government's austerity measures sparked a general strike in 1926.[5]

The United States had been the major beneficiary of the war's crippling effects on the European great powers. It was now the world's largest economy and the major international creditor. But the United States failed to adopt the kind of policies that would have allowed a return to stable economic growth internationally. It hoarded gold and ran a growing trade surplus, with a deflationary impact on the money supply in other countries. It raised tariffs on imports into the United States, making it harder for European borrowers to earn the US dollars they needed to repay their debts. And, ignoring the pleas of John Maynard Keynes to implement debt relief, it insisted on the repayment of crushing Allied war debts and German reparations in full.[6] American lending to the Europeans was fickle too. US capital flows had helped restore European economies early in the 1920s. But the booming American economy later in the decade pulled American investment back home, leaving Europeans high and dry.

Following the Wall Street Crash of 1929, the world economy ground to a halt. The United States raised interest rates to stabilize the dollar's value as the stock market plummeted. This only further provoked the collapse of banks and the contraction of the economy by stemming the supply of money just when it was needed most. American financing to the defeated Germany and Austria dried up and left them unable to meet their debt payments to the Allies. Bank failures followed. As financial panic spread throughout the international economy countries reacted with drastic measures. Controls on the movement of currency and restrictions on trade proliferated. Germany implemented strict controls on foreign capital movements and veered towards an autarkic policy of national socialism. Japan's economy was devastated by the effects of the Depression as prices for its key international export, rice, collapsed.[7] Britain abandoned the gold standard in 1931 and then sheltered behind its imperial markets through tariffs implemented at the Ottawa Agreement of 1932.[8] The liberal economic order lay in tatters. It was within these conditions that political extremism flourished and increasing nationalist and militaristic rivalry from the Axis powers (Italy, Germany, and Japan) drove the world into a second catastrophic war in twenty years.

This time is different

So how similar are today's dynamics to those of the 1930s? Firstly, in terms of the type of economic conditions since the Global Financial Crisis, things are very different. The economic crash that followed the banking crisis of 2007/8 was not of the same magnitude as the Great Depression. Except for Greece in the Eurozone, unemployment, deprivation, and desperation have not reached levels witnessed during the 1930s. Learning the lessons of the Depression, governments intervened to nationalize stricken banks and prevent the collapse of the financial system. And unlike the Federal Reserve's policy response of raising interest rates in 1929, this time the Fed and the world's other major central banks turned to monetary loosening through Quantitative Easing – boosting the money supply to stop the flow of credit from drying up. In China too, the government took measures to boost the credit supply and keep growth going.[9]

That governments and central banks were able to do this was thanks to another important difference. Outside of the European Union, most major currencies (like sterling, the dollar, and the yen) were floating and not fixed to one another. Unlike the gold standard, interest rates and the money supply could now be adjusted without fearing that a commitment to fixed currency values would be jeopardized. And unlike the gold standard, there was no legal requirement for a gold-backed domestic money supply. Credit could be created at will to ease the deflationary effects of the crisis. This was not, though, the case in the Eurozone where the shared currency meant that countries were much more restricted in how they could respond to the crisis. Only when the ECB belatedly stepped in to supply credit did the situation improve.

The level of international financial cooperation

between major governments, led by the United States through forums like the IMF and the newly created G20, enabled concerted action to prevent the onset of a new depression. This speaks to another important difference – the embedded liberal and neoliberal eras of globalization had led to much stronger multilateral arenas for dealing with global economic governance. That was not the case during the classical liberal and inter-war periods. Policy responses then were less well coordinated and global economic governance was much weaker. Globalization then looked very different from globalization now.

A similar argument applies to trade too. The liberal trading system that broke down during the 1930s was much more fragile than it is today. Protectionism had been on the increase in the final decades of the nineteenth century as late developing countries adopted economically nationalist policies. And as we saw in the previous chapter, much of the support for free trade in major economies was opportunistic and weak rather than doctrinaire or deeply rooted. There was no equivalent to the binding rules-based system that the WTO presides over today. And there were no regional free trade zones comparable to the EU, the Association of Southeast Asian Nations (ASEAN), or the North American Free Trade Agreement (NAFTA).

Within the nineteenth-century order, colonized peripheral supply zones had continued to play a major role in fuelling world economic growth. This was an imperial age as much as a liberal one. The more direct politicization of trade relations, given that they depended often on formal or informal control over foreign territories, made it much easier for the trade order to unravel under the pressure of rival imperialisms driven by expansionary European and Asian nationalism. The separation of the political and economic that characterizes liberal thinking about the world economy was not well established in practice during an era of imperial domination over colonized and subordinated countries. Many liberal thinkers in Britain actually defended the maintenance of Empire.[10] Economic influence abroad often meant territorial and political control. Where the two were fused, economic rivalry could rapidly morph into military conflict.

To understand why a 1930s-style scenario of rival economic spheres of influence, protectionism, and controls on capital is less likely today we also need to think about how feasible it would be to put such a system in place. The globalized production system of today illustrates just how difficult this would be. In the modern world economy, many goods are produced through 'global value chains' spanning across multiple different countries.[11] These value chains are coordinated by giant Multinational Corporations like Nike and Toyota, and they trade huge amounts *within* their own fragmented production process. Whereas the multinational firms of the first era of globalization tended to manufacture goods in one foreign country and then export the finished goods to others, today's multinationals have dispersed much more of their production, services, and sales capacities across a wider range of foreign markets. Rather than exporting goods produced in one foreign economy into all the rest, these firms establish production and distribution across these former export markets. This broader and deeper form of multinational production has gone hand in hand with a massive increase in foreign investment. By 2006, the total stock of global FDI was valued at $12 trillion. The firms involved are also much larger. Walmart, the world's largest firm in 2018, employed a workforce roughly equal to Norway's working population and had a turnover greater than Norwegian GDP.[12]

Global value chains now account for a staggering 80 per cent of world trade. That means that any serious disruption to them, by a return to the kinds of beggar-thy-neighbour policies put in place during the 1930s that prevented the movement of goods and capital across borders, would be hugely disruptive for the world economy. It could spark recession and unemployment. And because trade now matters more for most national economies, having increased from nine per cent of GDP in 1960 to 26.5 per cent by 2016 even for a large continental-scale economy like the United States, the domestic economic and political costs of these moves would be extreme. Any project looking to do this is likely to rapidly lose its political support base, particularly among the deep pockets of big business.

The global division of labour that Adam Smith famously endorsed in *The Wealth of Nations* is now much broader and deeper than ever before. More national economies have specialized around making a particular contribution to world trade. And more sectors within these national economies are now dependent upon global trade and investment for their survival. It is also a more consensual division of labour. It no longer relies upon nineteenth-century-style colonialism. Instead, national governments in developing countries around the world, albeit often under duress from the IMF and their Western creditors, have signed up to

policies opening up to the global economy. Political inequality and Northern domination of Southern countries
still exists, but there is much more formal independence for these countries than there was in the previous
era of globalization. This is particularly true when we
think about the trajectory of hugely powerful emerging
economies like India and China. Their rise has given the
Global South a much more powerful voice in governing the global economy. All of these factors mean that
economic self-sufficiency is now much harder and the
costs of disintegration correspondingly higher. In all of
the areas discussed above the depth and breadth of the
globalized condition are much greater.

There are also a number of important political and
cultural reasons for the greater staying power of contemporary globalization. The rise of fascism in Italy and
Germany occurred in a context of fragile democratic
systems that had only recently been established. And
from Italy to Germany and Japan, these remained conservative and traditional societies. All three states were
also working through the consequences of either late
national unification and/or rapid modernization from
feudal to capitalist societies that had only occurred
in the final third of the nineteenth century. Modern
democracies are more widespread and more deeply
established in many parts of the world. They are, of
course, not invulnerable. But the fragility or absence
of democratic structures in the 1930s and the lack of
any pervasive grip of the democratic imaginary over the
popular mindset, made the speedy rise of authoritarian
projects much easier.

Added to this was the peculiar legacy of the First
World War and the widespread disaffection that resulted

from the Treaty of Versailles. The terms of agreement reached in the Treaty were deeply unpopular with many states. Wilson's Fourteen Points and the emergence of a new world order under Anglo-American leadership were widely interpreted as a threat to other powers.[13] Germany resented the onerous burden of reparations, the 'war guilt clause' that allocated it the responsibility for the war, and the emasculation of German military power through the disarmament insisted upon by the French. In Italy and Japan too, the feeling was that Versailles had not properly recognized the territorial entitlements and respect that these rising powers should expect.

Versailles was not the only important legacy of the war. There was also an ingrained militarism within countries that had taken part in the war. This militarism is largely absent from the much more pacified international order of today. Beyond recent American and British forays into Iraq and Afghanistan in pursuit of regime change, the list of national armies engaged in serious conflict today is extremely limited. And the numbers enlisted into modern warfare are much more modest. This is important because fascism drew on the experience of the millions of traumatized soldiers that had suffered during the war and returned to their societies afterwards having been shaped by martial culture. Hitler himself had served in the war and considered his experiences in the trenches as formative to his toxic political project. A culture of militarism is also much more dangerous in the nuclear age. Escalation of conflict beyond a certain point is likely to lead to utter devastation with nuclear armed powers involved. This makes the possibility of a strategic victory inescapably Pyrrhic.

Why we are not in the 1930s

Back to the 1970s?

If not to the 1930s then where should we look to understand what is happening to contemporary globalization?
The 1970s is actually a more useful comparison. This
was the second major crisis of the globalization project
and, much like today, it also witnessed the growth of
political extremism. From the late 1960s, anarchists
blew up politicians in West Germany and Italy, while
the neo-Nazi National Front marched on the streets in
Britain.[14] In the United States, National Guards shot
down students protesting the Vietnam war in cold blood
on the Kent State campus. Political parties split further
along left-right lines. But the crisis did not lead to the
collapse of the open world economy. Much like today,
the reassertion of American national interests over the
established rules of the international economy caused
widespread disruption. Nixon's unilateral decision to
end Bretton Woods in 1971 and implement protectionist measures shook the global economy and shocked the
United States' allies. Deep economic malaise gripped
the world economy, with high inflation and low economic growth (stagflation) rocking confidence in the
post-war Keynesian accord. As the post-war consensus
about how to manage the economy and balance between
domestic and international priorities disintegrated,
a period of intense political struggle over the future
of the global economy began.[15] Developing countries
launched an ambitious plan to rewrite the rules of the
international economy and the tumultuous politics of
the Middle East, as well as the formation of a new cartel
of oil producing countries (OPEC), pushed up oil prices

and slowed world economic growth. Strikes increased dramatically throughout the West as class conflict intensified. Cultural changes led to deep dissatisfaction with the rhythms of post-war life and inspired the flowering of youth revolts against established power.

Despite all of these challenges the world economy held together. Even though Nixon severed the dollar's link to gold, there was no widespread turn to protectionism and capital controls as there had been when the gold standard collapsed during the 1930s. After a period of turbulence in the financial markets, agreements were reached about how to move forward. Financial liberalization continued apace, and global financial markets grew rapidly. The trade order did not collapse and by the 1980s the movement towards freer trade had recovered its momentum. And the United States, despite facing deep economic and political problems during the decade, continued to act as the fulcrum around which the global economy turned. The dollar's role as the dominant international currency proved secure with the United States at the centre of global financial markets.

This happened because the foundations of globalization were much stronger than they had been before. Major economies were more dependent on trade and had become more deeply interconnected through the international financial system. For major export powerhouses like Japan and West Germany, hosts to powerful coalitions of exporters, it simply didn't make sense to abandon free trade and close in on themselves. They needed continued access to the US market and continued use of the dollar as the dominant international currency. The United States in the 1970s was not Britain in the 1930s. It remained overwhelmingly dominant in

economic and military terms. Nor was the turn to protected imperialist spheres to underwrite autarky really
feasible in an age when decolonization had been set in
train and Western international relations had been pacified through NATO. The undisputed military supremacy
of the United States within the West and the Cold War
antagonism with the Soviet Union made major independent geopolitical ambitions practically impossible and
politically undesirable. Europe responded to the crisis
with deeper trade and monetary integration through the
European Economic Community.

Thinking about the crisis of the 1970s can shed some
light on what is happening today. Of course, history can
only provide a rough guide to the present, not a mirror
image. Not all of these forces are playing out today.
Oil prices have remained low since the crisis and the
main problem for many economies has been deflation
rather than inflation. And in an age of defeated labour
movements and declining trade union membership, the
major strike activity seen in the 1970s has been absent.
But there is a common thread that links US policy under
Nixon and Trump. In retrospect, the policies of the
United States under Nixon could be seen more as a
haphazard attempt to reset the global economy in line
with changing American national interests rather than
an attempt to provoke global disintegration. The 1970s
came to represent the end of the embedded liberal vision
of globalization, not the end of globalization *tout court*.

This parallel can help us understand the politics of
Donald Trump in the United States. Trump is certainly
not Nixon. His advocacy of white supremacy is uniquely
intense and disturbing. He has praised white nation-
alists, referred to Mexicans as rapists, and repeatedly

represented black politicians and celebrities as having low IQs. His erratic and combative manner of communication via Twitter, and his disdain for the constraints implied by governing in a democracy, are also without precedent. We should be very alarmed about what Donald Trump means both for the future of the United States and the wider world. Trump's tough stance on international trade has provoked particularly strong concerns and is at the forefront of fears that the United States is about to renounce globalization. His administration has undermined the WTO by blocking the appointment of judges to the Appellate Court, where countries meet to resolve disputes over a range of trade issues.[16] Bypassing the WTO, Trump's administration has favoured bilateral trade bargaining with both the European Union and China. And by threatening to impose sanctions unilaterally on China for violating American intellectual property rights, Trump has further undermined the multilateral basis for resolving trade disputes.[17]

Yet Trump's attempt to drive a hard bargain through trade, in resorting to protectionist measures against those he considers to be abusing America, does have a precedent. Since the end of the Second World War, US elites' support for globalization has been based on the understanding that it furthers American national interests. If, rightly or wrongly, the American electorate and political class begin to see a disjuncture between globalization and American interests then political and economic strategies challenging globalization become more popular. American politicians know that the status of the United States at the heart of the global economy, like Britain in the nineteenth century but with greater power and influence, gives them unusual scope to attempt to rewrite the rulebook. Using the carrot of access to American markets and finance, and the stick of protectionist measures and tough talk, they try to bend global economic relations towards their interests. Economic policy is and has always been closely linked to American geopolitical ambitions too, with sanctions and tariffs imposed on enemies of the US regime. Other countries accept these measures because they recognize that playing by American rules allows them access to an integrated global economic system underwritten by American financial and military power. In other words, the United States provides certain public goods for the system as a whole. And in the absence of American commitment to globalization, whatever the caveats to that commitment might be, there is simply no clear alternative for how to organize the global economy.

Of course, not all of Trump's hostility towards the current trade order reflects a strategic calculus to improve trade agreements in America's interests. Politics is much messier than that. And Trump's ponderous intellect is undeserving of such consistently rational attribution. Politically, Trump and his advisors are also playing to his electoral base, with tariffs on steel imports a clear sop to the steel-town swing states that brought him to power. While most Americans are opposed to increased tariffs, the majority of Republican voters favour them.[18] So there is a clear electoral logic to this. But within Trump's approach to trade the more traditional aspect of American policy towards globalization can also be seen. This is echoed by the economic philosophy of Trump's trade representative Robert Lighthizer. Lighthizer has rapidly become the most influential voice on trade in Washington DC. His philosophy is unabashedly pro-free trade. Where he differs from the previous orthodoxy is in his desire to use a wide range of explicitly politicized bargaining tools to achieve those free trade goals. To do this, Lighthizer prefers a divide and conquer bilateral negotiation approach (rather than multilateral) that allows US leverage to be brought to bear on individual trade partners.[19] Again, such an approach by the United States is not without precedent in recent American history. Ronald Reagan similarly used what has been referred to as 'aggressive unilateralism' to achieve US trade goals by threatening US protectionist measures against countries that America perceived as maintaining unfair trade practices.[20]

This approach is clearly visible in the recent disputes with the EU, Canada, and Mexico. After threatening major tariffs on EU exports to the United States, Trump agreed to halt plans to impose new tariffs and declared a 'new phase' of transatlantic trade relations after meeting with Jean-Claude Juncker, the President of the European Commission, in July 2018. Trump and Juncker swerved away from what looked like a budding trade war to announce plans to eliminate tariffs on all non-auto industrial goods, increase cooperation on energy purchases, and pursue reform of the WTO. The United States won important concessions from the EU, with the Europeans agreeing to increase US soybean and liquefied natural gas imports.[21]

Trump's trade policy represents a high stakes game of chicken, echoing Nixon's sentiment that, 'the more you risk if you lose, the more you stand to gain if you win'.[22] In his efforts to renegotiate NAFTA Trump has exhibited a similar approach. In August 2017, he used his Twitter account to publicly criticize the obstinate position adopted by Canada and Mexico, suggesting that the United States might have to terminate the agreement.[23] But by October 2018, Trump had reached a renewed trade agreement with Mexico and Canada in the form of the 'United States–Mexico–Canada–Agreement' (USMCA). The new deal is likely to bring some production back to the United States and Canada by stipulating that a minimum input must be added in factories that pay their workers at least $16 per hour. In terms of rules of origin, which codify what percentage of inputs imported from outside are allowed for goods made within the region to benefit from the trade agreement, the new deal has made these rules more demanding for car makers by raising the required percentage of regional auto production from 62.5 per cent to 75 per cent. It also opens up the protected Canadian dairy market to US imports. Finally, the United States has successfully pressed for a break clause after sixteen years, at which point the deal will expire and need to be renegotiated.[24] Trump is a businessman. He approaches politics much like he approaches business – courting corruption and bending the rules when it suits his interests, using his leverage and going right to the wire to drive the hardest bargain possible.

Trump's hardline stance on China is also not hugely surprising when we recognize that US elites have long considered the Chinese their most credible challenger for global supremacy. The US trade deficit has been a perennial bugbear for hawks within the US administration.[25] It was always likely that confidence in the merits of an uneasy Sino-American economic interdependence would weaken as the power gap between the two countries narrowed. American elites have long feared that

China's massive holdings of US dollar assets, built up by running a long-term trade surplus with the United States, give China leverage over US economic policy. And with China now catching-up and in some cases overtaking the United States in leading-edge sectors like AI and robotics, there are fears that the US military advantage will be steadily eroded. These concerns do not belong only to Trump. Business interests are increasingly worried about integration with Chinese supply-chains in the case of a potential military show-down over the South China Sea.[26] Economic interests and national security are drawing closer together as American anxieties about Chinese power intensify.

Trade tensions between the United States and China are also likely to prove more intractable because this is in many ways a disagreement about the Chinese state-led model of capitalism. Washington believes that China's unique economy gives it an unfair advantage in international trade and leads to a host of uncompetitive practices that distort trade in the Chinese interest. China's unique economic model has left it awkwardly misaligned with WTO treaty law, meaning that the WTO can only deal with a limited range of (the numerous) disputes in which China's policies are close enough to those of other countries and the foundations of international trade law.[27] Trump's pressure on both the WTO and China directly needs to be read in this context, with the main trade advisor to the White House, Peter Navarro, a vocal exponent of a hawkish approach to China on trade and foreign policy. This kind of deepening rivalry between the United States and China might lead to decreased trade and economic integration between the two. But it is unlikely to lead to wholesale 'deglobalization'. A more regionally clustered but still highly interconnected global economy is more likely, with China increasingly central in Asia and the United States still dominant in the Western hemisphere. And in any case, globalization has always been based around strong regional projects of trade and financial integration.

What about the other major shock to the globalization project in recent years, the UK's vote for Brexit? Brexit has been interpreted as a rejection of the cosmopolitan liberal economic vision by the disenchanted and disaffected losers of globalization. The Leave Campaign's message to 'take back control' from an alien European bureaucracy resonated with those who felt disempowered by the forces of global markets and the European Union's democratically hollow logic of supranational political integration. Anti-immigrant rhetoric and an appeal to restore the integrity of Britain's borders tapped into xenophobia linked to economic and cultural anxiety. Brexit clearly does represent a major threat to a central pillar of contemporary globalization – the deep economic and political integration represented by the EU.

Understanding Brexit as a straightforward renunciation of globalization would, though, be deeply misleading. Yes, the popular support for it, particularly among lower-income groups, can partially be understood that way. But Brexit was also supported by affluent metropolitan voters in parts of southern England. It is at least in part a rejection of the particular form of political integration of the European Union, which has involved compromising parliamentary sovereignty over EU regulatory competences and the European Court of Justice. This rubs against deeply held beliefs of parliamentary sovereignty and a post-imperial nostalgia for the singular autonomy of the United Kingdom – a state that violated the sovereignty of those under its imperial jurisdiction rather than accepting limits on its own powers. Voting to reject this specific project of integration is not the same as voting against globalization, although the effect of the former may be to hasten the demise of the latter. The motivations for Brexit are complicated and multiple. They are not reducible to a single cause. A desire to reaffirm national sovereignty against encroachment from supranational institutions or flows of migrants is a common thread. It is evidence that deeper forms of globalization can provoke a backlash that looks to reaffirm the power of the nation state and regain control over political and economic forces.

To properly understand Brexit, though, we need to disentangle popular motivations from those of the Conservative Party elite and to disentangle anti-European sentiment from anti-globalization sentiment. Elite motivations for Brexit from within the Conservative Party are very different from those expressed by the electorate. Leave voters and Conservative politicians are bonded by a common disdain for the European Union. But Tory hardliners like Daniel Hannan, Liam Fox, and Jacob Rees-Mogg, all keen advocates of Brexit, actually view it as an opportunity to increase free trade and widen the global reach of Britain's trading relationship. Viewed from the perspective of trade, this is a demand for more globalization, not less. For a 'Global Britain' rather than a Britain that conducts almost half of its international trade with the European Union.

What the troubled negotiations over Brexit already

demonstrate is just how hard it will be to extricate from deep forms of economic integration associated with globalization. Business leaders have railed against the threat to European supply-chains and the declining appeal of Britain as a recipient of vitally needed FDI. The City of London is striving for a Brexit that maintains its status as a premier global financial centre and home for major transnational financial institutions. Britain's economy is one of the most heavily internationalized advanced economies in the world. Across almost every sector of the economy, there is a need for continuing close links to Europe. Bespoke sectoral arrangements to maintain access to the European Union's markets and resources will likely limit the eventual severity of Britain's departure, from financial services to higher education. Much as in the 1970s, the centripetal forces holding economic interdependence together are strong and deeply embedded within a range of national and supranational institutions. This makes the costs of disintegration much higher and the politics of achieving it much more complex and messier. In practice, then, Brexit may prove to be an ideal type rather than a genuine disentanglement from all forms of European political and economic integration. Looked at from the vantage point of free-trade Conservatives enamoured with the idea of 'Global Britain', this is, much like elements of Trump's international economic policy, about renegotiating rather than renouncing the terms and conditions of contemporary globalization.

The picture on trade is, then, more complicated than it might first appear. Trump and Brexit do not entail a full-blooded rejection of free trade. Trump has used the threat of protectionism as leverage with regard to major trading partners like the EU, then doubled down on free trade once appropriate concessions have been made. And with regard to China, rising geopolitical rivalry has long been a simmering threat to Sino-American economic interdependence, regardless of the wider popular mood towards globalization. In Britain, Conservative advocates of Brexit ultimately want more, not less, free trade. And they want it with a more, not less, global set of partners. Added to that, the motivations for the changing politics of free trade within the US and British governments are very different. The United States fears China's rise and wants to make life more difficult economically for its potential peer competitor. The British government, conversely, is using the rise of emerging markets like China and India to push for more free trade and greater regional diversification.

With regard to another crucial driver of globalization, the flow of capital across borders, it is difficult to identify an anti-globalization consensus. Unlike the 1930s, Trump and the Brexiteers have made zero noise about restricting international capital flows. In fact, Trump has been a keen advocate of deregulating Wall Street and undoing some of the restrictions put in place after the financial crisis. And the right-wing media in Britain have called for greater liberalization of financial services in Britain after Brexit.[28] Speaking at the Conservative Party Conference in October 2017, then Foreign Secretary and key Brexiteer Boris Johnson suggested that there were 'massive opportunities for this country to be a leader and campaign for liberalization of trade in services'.[29]

If globalization is not completely unravelling under the pressure of political shocks like Trump and Brexit, then this raises an important question. What *is* going on? What we are witnessing is a crisis of a certain phase of globalization. A crisis of the neoliberal vision of globalization set in train at the end of the 1970s that stripped away the uneasy balance between domestic and international priorities set in place after the Second World War. Deepening inequality, ecological devastation, increased migration, and a sense of declining national control over political and economic outcomes has produced popular anger and disaffection. This disaffection has been cynically manipulated by self-serving elites around the world. But the right-wing political response to this crisis actually threatens to make the situation much worse.

By continuing down the road of free capital markets and freer trade, while clamping down on the free movement of people and peddling divisive racist discourses, a newly ascendant national liberalism threatens to sow the seeds for further disappointment and anger. This may generate much darker forces of political and economic disintegration. The deeper condition of contemporary globalization provides breathing space to prevent this, raising the costs and obstacles to renouncing globalization. But it also means that if reactionary forces continue to speak the language of popular empowerment, while doubling down on policies that have generated widespread dissatisfaction, the forces of regressive disintegration will become much stronger and the consequences of their potential triumph far worse.

4

Neoliberalism unravelling

Zuccotti Park is a large open space in the heart of New York's Wall Street financial district. In September 2011 it became the home of the Occupy Wall Street movement. Thousands of protesters gathered in the square to challenge the dominance of America's financial sector. They highlighted the staggering inequality that has become the hallmark of contemporary capitalism. The protesters coined a simple slogan – 'We are the 99 per cent.' It referred to the massive income and wealth disparities that had developed, since the 1980s, between the top percentile of the income distribution and the rest – the gap between the winners of globalization and the losers.

The Occupy movement was part of a global wave of political protest and ideological polarization that took root in the wake of the financial crisis. It symbolized the decay of the popular political consensus underpinning neoliberalism – the ideology that has governed the most expansionary and intense period of globalization. Over the past decade, neoliberalism has been challenged from both the left and the right. The demands for democratic renewal and progressive economic redistribution represented by the Occupy movement have gradually been drowned out by reactionary support for illiberal politics and authoritarian rulers. Populist parties and leaders, stoking nativist fears of immigration and mobilizing economic discontent, have attacked the values of tolerance, pluralism, and openness that are the lifeblood of democracy.

As the global economy stuttered and stalled in the wake of the crisis, the deep fault lines opened up by the rapid expansion of globalization cracked through the surface of contemporary politics. The restored priority of free trade and free capital flows under neoliberalism, and the rolling back of the welfare state commitments of the post-war period, have had damaging effects. Spiralling inequality, financial instability, increased geographical divisions between the winners and losers of globalization, economic austerity, and a widespread loss of faith in the promise of democratic governments have transformed the political landscape. Added to this, the rapid economic catch-up by emerging economies has provoked anxiety within the West. The foundations of contemporary globalization have been shaken.

But, despite these problems, the unique depth of today's globalized condition has meant that the world economy has not disintegrated. It also means that there is a long road yet to walk, both politically and economically, before a situation of genuine deglobalization becomes plausible. There are simply too many forms of deep economic interdependence and integration for this to happen without an extremely sustained and concerted political attack on the foundations of our interconnected world economy. The crisis of the neoliberal era of globalization needs to be understood within this context.

There is, nonetheless, plenty of cause for alarm. The depth and breadth of the globalized condition buys time to reconfigure globalization on a more sustainable basis. It strengthens the prospect of salvaging a cosmopolitan international order based on democratic values and institutions within and between nation states. But it also means that the costs of disintegration, should it occur, may be much higher than experienced before. The dominant exclusionary nationalist and socially illiberal reaction to the crisis of globalization is extremely dangerous. And it is gathering momentum. A new balance of political forces has begun to crystallize. One that, if left unchallenged, possesses the potential to unravel the globalized condition with devastating consequences. To avoid this, progressive forces will have to develop a strong narrative and powerful political coalitions to rebuild a democratic and egalitarian project within states. Only stronger domestic foundations can give the global economy a more sustainable basis. The project for building a better world economy has to begin at home.

Throughout the Western heartland of the globalization project there is a rising nationalist challenge. We are witnessing the emergence of a toxic 'national liberalism'. But unlike previous liberal doctrines for shaping globalization this is not a bold new vision with a coherent blueprint. It is a messy phase of political contestation that has been spawned by the crises and limits of the neoliberal vision of globalization – intensified global competition, sharper income polarization between the winners and losers of globalization, social alienation, and the hollowing out of popular democratic sovereignty inaugurated by neoliberalism's aggressive project to restore the dominance of the market over society. National liberalism is the nascent ideology of a period that threatens global disintegration. It represents the political, economic, and ecological exhaustion of the market-liberal vision for how to organize the global economy.

National liberalism mobilizes an increasingly racist, exclusionary, and xenophobic discourse of resentment that challenges liberal social values and cosmopolitan ethics. Yet it offers no compelling vision for how to make globalization work for the common good. And it offers no compelling critique of the structures of contemporary capitalism. Structures that have generated increasing dissatisfaction with the status quo. This is why it is so dangerous. Citizens have been mobilized by politicians willing to stoke the flames of anti-immigrant sentiment and restore the priority of the nation. But those same politicians have, either by choice (in Britain and the United States) or necessity (within the context of the EU's constitutionalized pro-market structures), largely retained the commitment to free trade, free capital flows, and the free market that have been central to the social and economic dislocation caused by neoliberal globalization. National liberalism does not properly address the economic dimensions of political dissatisfaction. Instead it directs discontent towards an increasingly racist and xenophobic approach to controlling another key feature of globalization – migratory flows. National liberalism seeks to restore and appease demands for national sovereignty through targeting migrants as a deviant strand of contemporary globalization to be controlled through tighter borders. The threat of this current partial repudiation of liberalism, which maintains conviction in the power of the market while challenging cosmopolitan values, is that it may spur a much more dangerous form of exclusionary economic and political nationalism. This might, in time, lead to a much more destructive form of global disintegration. Progressive solutions to the crisis of globalization are urgently needed.

Global fault lines

The intellectual vision championed by the disciples of the Mont Pelerin Society has had devastating effects. Stripped of its commitments to full employment, capital controls, and a generous cushion of welfare provision, the globalization project has steadily eroded popular support. The financial crisis represented the global instability brought about by a world of liberalized and enlarged global capital flows. But it also acted as a catalyst, energizing political responses to a deeper set of problems that have blighted contemporary capitalism. In doing so it fractured the political consensus around the neoliberal project. The measures used to try to deal with the consequences of the crisis, from fiscal austerity to loose monetary policy, have failed to quell rising political opposition. They have not been able to secure political legitimacy for contemporary capitalism. Domestically, governments throughout the world have struggled to maintain their grip on power within a context of weaker economic performance and political polarization. While internationally, the momentum towards further globalization has ebbed away as American leadership has been withdrawn.

How do we make sense of what is behind the crisis of globalization? We need to think about the interaction of two different types of problems that are shaping contemporary politics. The first type of problem is of a longer-term and more structural character. These are problems that emerge from the DNA of neoliberal globalization as a project. They include the changing geography of global inequality, both within and between countries, the uneven economic performance of different countries within the world market, declining levels of economic productivity and growth, and environmental devastation. There is a strong element of inevitability surrounding the emergence of these problems, given the particular way that globalization has been designed and implemented by political and business elites. Overcoming them means rethinking how we organize and govern globalization.

These problems have interacted with a second type of problem. Problems that are of a more contingent nature in terms of their relationship to the structural problems outlined above. These problems are less directly a product of neoliberal globalization. They were not an inevitable consequence of neoliberalism and might well have arisen without it. Their emergence alongside these deep structural problems is coincidental. They include issues like the refugee crisis that emerged from the civil war in Syria and the Islamophobia that has been generated by the War on Terror (long pre-dating the financial crisis). Although linked to the changes brought about by globalization, these problems cannot be reduced to a single dominant cause or viewed as internal to liberal visions of political economy.

It is the timing of the combination between these deep-rooted structural problems and more contingent dilemmas that has framed current political responses to the crisis and fuelled right-wing populism. The ascendancy of the right-wing response to the crisis of neoliberal globalization is not simply a consequence of the weakness of progressive forces. It is also a response to the coincidence of the legacy of the economic crisis (the austerity, diminished living standards, and general mood of political defeatism it led to) with unusually intense mass movements by migrants and refugees shaped by geopolitical events in the Middle East. This is certainly the case in Europe. In the United States, the right-wing reaction has much to do with the racial anxiety prompted among whites by the presidency of Barack Obama and fears of a changing demographic balance.

Starting with the first type of problem, what are the major design flaws of neoliberal globalization and what effects have they had? The changing pattern of global inequality is a good place to begin. The Occupy movement helped raise the political salience of inequality. But the political effects of inequality have been deeper and broader than the emergence of protest movements. Looking at the global distribution of inequality helps us understand why popular support for globalization has weakened in the West, while strengthening in major emerging powers like China and India.

First the good news – when we take the weighting of populations within countries into account, rather than simply comparing countries, inequality has actually

declined during the peak phase of globalization since
the 1980s. Because of the rapid economic development
of vastly populous countries like China, India, and
Indonesia, hundreds of millions of people have escaped
poverty.[1] This is undoubtedly a good thing and should
be recognized as a benefit of globalization.

But when we look at inequality *within* rather than
between countries, a different picture emerges. This is
the story of the rise of the top one per cent (even top
0.1 per cent) relative to all of the rest. Declining global
inequality *between* countries has been combined with
deepening inequality *within* countries. The big winners
from globalization have been the top one per cent of the
global income distribution, whose incomes rose by a
staggering 60 per cent over two decades, and the 'emerging global middle classes', who saw even larger gains of
between 60 and 80 per cent. The losers have been the
75th to 90th percentiles – the middle classes within the
advanced economies.

What is driving this starkly polarized tendency within
the distribution of income? The intensification of trade
and financial liberalization from the 1980s has had
important distributional effects that have reshaped patterns of global income inequality. As more developing
countries were brought into the world market, and as
financial liberalization allowed greater foreign investment by advanced countries' MNCs, a vast number
of unskilled and low-skilled workers entered into the
world economy. The landmark event was China's entry
into the world market, crowned by its accession to the
WTO in December 2001. Competition intensified both
between workers in advanced and developed economies,
and between workers within developed countries, as

projects such as the European single market integrated financial and labour markets.[2]

All of this dragged down wages and deepened the international division of labour. Labour-intensive sectors were relocated in developing countries, while developed countries increasingly specialized in capital intensive, high-skilled, and high-tech work. For developing countries this meant rising wages for those tapping into the new division of labour and moving from the countryside to the urban areas. But for the advanced economies the outcome was very different. The wages of lower skilled workers in the West dropped while wages of those in the higher-end activities increased, deepening income inequality within the West. Not only this, but skilled workers in the West also lost out. Innovations in IT and communications meant that even skilled tasks could be relocated – think customer service call centres in Mumbai. The security of employment in the West also declined as manufacturing jobs were offshored or replaced by new technology. Globalization helped to rapidly accelerate deindustrialization within the West, devastating industrial regions that had no alternative sources of well-paid employment.[3]

Within both developed and developing countries, despite the growth in wages for workers in the South, inequality has intensified. This is because the biggest beneficiary of neoliberal globalization has been global capital – the owners of the assets used in production and other economic activity. Western MNCs have relocated production to lower-wage economies to increase their returns on investment. While a rising class of capitalists in China and India have experienced massive increases in their income by driving integration with the world market.[4] Greater integration of the global economy led to higher global growth rates from the 1980s, but its impacts were highly uneven – benefiting the rising middle class in some major developing countries more than the stagnant lower middle classes in the West. The benefits of globalization bypassed some economies, like those of sub-Saharan Africa, altogether, while boosting the incomes of the owners of capital globally. When we look at the distribution of wealth too, there is a clear picture of increasing concentration at the top globally, among a small but expanding group of global billionaires.[5]

Some of these changes were the consequence of the general ebb and flow of global income and wealth linked to the way that countries in the global economy rise and fall over time. But many of the effects were driven by policy decisions informed by neoliberal ideas. Financial liberalization swelled financial markets and boosted financial sector income. Tax cuts for the rich reduced the redistributive capacity of states while greater financial integration allowed offshore centres to cloak taxable revenue. Privatization and deregulation boosted the incomes of those capturing formerly public assets, often at fire sale prices. Changing labour market policies and anti-union laws led to lower union membership density and reduced workers' share of national income. In the Global South, structural adjustment programmes implemented under the Washington Consensus deepened inequality.

The political consequences of changing patterns of global inequality have been aggravated by declining rates of economic growth since the financial crisis. Growth in the West stalled spectacularly. Output fell by up to nine per cent in some major economies and growth didn't return to pre-crisis levels for years. Wages stagnated, and investment dropped sharply.[6] Western economic malaise was a particularly acute feature of a wider decline of global growth. Even China's rapid growth rate declined from over 15 per cent at its pre-crisis peak, to below seven per cent by 2018. The same is true for many of the emerging markets, which experienced a steep drop in the prices of their key commodity exports after the crisis.[7] As growth rates decline, and incomes stagnate, distributional politics becomes more of a zero-sum game – the haves against the have-nots. Without the prospect of rising incomes through increased economic growth, existing inequalities appear locked in. And as growth rates slow and wages stagnate, higher rates of return on assets mean that those with greater access to wealth pull away from those dependent on income earned through employment.[8]

Policy responses to the crisis, informed by the reigning neoliberal ideology, aggravated these effects. After a brief flirtation with Keynesian demand-management policies, governments eschewed Keynesian policy and opted for fiscal austerity – curbing government spending and depressing demand within the economy.[9] This was in keeping with the way that neoliberals had argued against Keynesian strategies for achieving stable economic growth. This made the recession worse and contributed to stagnating incomes and declining investment. By 2016 even the IMF, long a bastion of neoliberal orthodoxy, urged governments to ease off.[10]

Having shunned a pro-active fiscal policy in response to the crisis, governments looked to monetary policy instead. Turning to ultra-low interest rates and

'Quantitative Easing', central banks attempted to boost economic demand via financial markets. They hoped that pushing up asset prices and creating a 'wealth effect' for asset holders would lead to greater spending and investment. Quantitative easing had regressive effects. It boosted the wealth of the small segment of the population that holds most of the financial assets.[11] Fiscal policies to boost wages and increase public investment would have enabled a more progressive response, raising wages for those lower down the wealth and income hierarchy and creating better public infrastructure and services. They might have also tackled the urgently needed investment required for setting the global economy on a greener environmental foundation. But these opportunities were not taken.

The slowing of growth around the world, and particularly within the wealthy advanced economies, provoked fears of 'secular stagnation' – a long-term decline in the rate of growth due to structural changes that reduced the appetite for investment in the economy and depressed demand. Proponents of this view have pointed to ageing populations, new 'capital conserving' businesses like Apple and Uber, and growing inequality as drivers of declining investment and growth.[12] Free-market policies have deepened the polarization of economic benefits, leading to a declining capacity to consume and drive growth due to stalled incomes among large parts of the population, while helping to centralize profits and investment potential in a smaller group of globally dominant corporations.

How to restore growth is a challenge that has wider dimensions than questions of how to raise investment and increase demand. A distinctive feature of the crisis of neoliberal globalization is that it is the first in which it is now widely understood that further growth, at least of the carbon-intensive, fossil fuel dependent form that has driven capitalism since the Industrial Revolution, is ecologically unsustainable. The limits of growth may have been reached, even breached. The prospects for returning to pre-crisis levels of growth in the long term look dismal. Unlike previous crises of globalization, restoring productivity and growth is no longer enough to reset globalization on a more sustainable basis. In the longer term, this is likely to prove the biggest challenge for recovering some form of globalization. More directly, the deep structural issues discussed above have interacted with a more immediate and contingent set of policy shocks to energize a wave of regressive populist politics in many parts of the world.

The populist challenge

The strangely synchronous election of Donald Trump as President of the United States and Britain's vote for Brexit in 2016 shocked the world. Trump's declared intention to put 'America first' and the Leave Campaign's slogan of 'taking back control' symbolized a shared desire to restore sovereignty and reassert the primacy of national interests. That these events occurred in the Anglo-American heartland of the globalization project made them particularly significant for signalling the changing political mood. They struck at two pillars of post-war globalization – American support for an open world economy, and the project of European integration.

Trump's election victory and Britain's vote to leave

the EU were motivated by distinctive underlying causes. But they also shared several crucial things in common. Trump won the election by decrying America's ruling elite and attempting to speak on behalf of the 'real' American people. In Britain, Nigel Farage's UK Independence Party (UKIP) was central to bringing about the Conservative government's decision to hold a referendum on European Union membership. Their electoral success pushed the Conservative government further to the right and sparked fears that disaffection to UKIP would weaken Conservative electoral dominance. Much like Trump, Farage denounced the role of corrupt European elites and the Brussels bureaucracy, declaring the referendum outcome of a vote to leave the EU as a 'victory for real people'.[13] The anti-elitism embodied by UKIP bled into a wider distrust of 'expert' knowledge that characterized the fractious and dismal referendum debate.

This common thread of anti-elitism and the rallying narrative of 'the pure people' against the 'corrupt elites' place the Anglo-American political shocks within a broader upsurge of populist politics. Populist politicians and parties are characterized by a simplistic moral vision of political life. A vision that pits a corrupt, morally compromised elite against the 'real' people. Populist politicians then make an *exclusive* claim that they, and only they, are capable of representing the people. This is the anti-pluralist strand to populism – the denial that any other politicians or parties are able to represent the people. And this is why populism is a danger to liberal democracy. The denial of the possibility that popular interests can be represented by anyone other than the populists themselves is incompatible with the liberal democratic premise of a competing field of different parties and politicians all able to make some legitimate claim to represent the wishes of the people. Anti-pluralism threatens to lead us down the road to authoritarianism. Worse still, in creating a binary distinction between the real people and everyone else, it risks the creation of marginalized 'others'. Those who are outside of the true body politic and not subject to the privileges and respect extended to the 'real' people.[14]

Although the content of populist politics since the financial crisis has varied across countries and regions, the form has been strikingly consistent. Time and time again, parties and politicians have denounced the corruption of incumbent elites and made sweeping claims to represent the people. Across Europe, populist leaders have risen to defend the interests of the people against the elites. Attacks against European elites and cosmopolitan globalists have linked populist leaders, from Beppe Grillo's Five Star Movement in Italy to Viktor Orban's Fidesz government in Hungary and the ruling Law and Justice Party (PiS) in Poland. In Turkey, Recep Tayyip Erdogan has described himself as a 'man of the people' and fuelled resentment against the 'Republican elites' charged with being disconnected from popular values. Rising to power in 2014, Narendra Modi's Bharatiya Janata Party has mobilized an aggressive Hindu nationalist discourse in India to rail against the threat posed by morally compromised elites embedded within Indian institutions.

Populism is not new. It has a long history within liberal democracy. Its rise is not only a consequence of globalization. It also reflects, particularly in the West, some of the hollowing out of democratic forms

96

of government in recent decades. Parties looked to monopolize a representative centre ground and became tightly integrated with and dependent upon the state. Party memberships declined along with voter turnout, and mainstream parties failed to capture their previous shares of the vote.[15] Populism has also been influenced by recent increases in migration and refugee flows that have prompted a nativist reaction from the UK, to Sweden, and Hungary.

Advanced globalization has, though, certainly played into this. The more rules-based and deeply institutionalized form of global economic integration brought about under neoliberalism has sapped some of the representative vitality from national democratic politics. Neoliberal thinkers sought to protect the operations of the market from democratic scrutiny.[16] Nowhere has this process of democratic sterilization been clearer than in the EU, where the constitutionalized pro-market order brought about by deep trade and financial integration has jarred with popular demands for national sovereignty and greater economic autonomy. The 'democratic deficit' that has long characterized the EU project leaves a widening disconnect between national politics and the Brussels political class. The failure of many developing countries to benefit from globalization has also led to increasing migration, with movement abroad more likely to enable increased income for the migrant than progression within a home economy in which incomes have stalled.[17]

At a time of economic stagnation and in a post-crisis period that has lifted the veil on German dominance within the EU, European countries have been particularly vulnerable to the populist challenge. Populist parties, highlighting issues and agendas neglected by mainstream parties but salient to discontented segments of the electorate, have occupied the gaps left by the crowding of the centre ground. They have been fuelled by the legitimacy void opened up by the transfer of power to democratically deficient EU institutions. They have used their anti-EU and anti-elite discourse as leverage to open up space and build a support base. And they have mobilized those who are dissatisfied with the bitter fruits of globalization. In a context of the deep structural problems associated with globalization, populist parties and politicians have been able to make rapid headway as the legitimacy of neoliberal globalization has disintegrated.

Although populism is by definition anti-pluralist, it is not necessarily right-wing. The nationalist and reactionary tone of contemporary populism needs to be explained. It is derived from two main sources. It is, firstly, a response to the deep structural changes brought about by neoliberal globalization. Inequality has created a fertile terrain of dissatisfaction and psychological anxiety. Geographical divisions have enabled populists to target areas that have not been able to share in the benefits of globalization, manipulating the metropolitan-periphery divide between global cities and post-industrial hinterlands with particular efficiency. China's rise and the increased growth of Brazil, Russia, India and China (the BRICs) has provoked anxiety in the West. And China's increased power within the global economy, alongside the geopolitical resurgence of Putin's Russia, has provided examples of the capability of authoritarian governments. This has challenged the international supremacy of liberalism. Demographic transformations, shaped by increased flows of people looking for better employment opportunities or fleeing war-torn regions in a more interconnected world, have provoked cultural anxiety and backlash among host populations.

As the deeper and broader form of globalization associated with the neoliberal era has rapidly transformed societies, the nation state has been politically reactivated and tasked with protecting the social and economic conditions of its population. This is part of the long-standing tension between the liberal universalism of the market order, and the endurance of the nation state as a space in which national and local claims are made against the uneven effects of global capitalism. Indeed, the neoliberal era has always contained a strong nationalist thread within it. In order to navigate the competitive international state system, neoliberal ideas have been mobilized through nationalist and conservative political projects. The Thatcher and Reagan administrations are exemplary in this regard. Both politicians sought to restore national pride and power. And they did so by targeting deviant strands within society, who were understood as threats to the moral integrity of the nation and the freedom of the market.[18] More broadly, neoliberals exhibit greater scepticism towards forms of cosmopolitan internationalism than do other liberals. Unless such forms are geared towards locking in constitutionalized commitments to the supremacy of the free market, neoliberals have frequently defended the primacy of national sovereignty as the surest means to maintain the reign of market forces.[19]

Attempts to re-energize the nation state as a political unit can be understood within the longer historical tensions between the universal world market and national geographies of political representation and power. But the specifically xenophobic and socially illiberal character of Western populism cannot. To understand that we need to think about the acute conditions that have shaped post-crisis politics. Anti-immigration sentiment has been a common thread of populist politics in the West. Even in a time of declining European economic performance, the continent has continued to attract large flows of migrants and asylum seekers. Capitalizing on increased resentment towards migrants and asylum seekers, populist national parties have gained ground, with nationalist governments formed in Hungary and Poland, alongside the entry of the racist Lega Nord party into a Coalition government with the Five Star Movement in Italy.[20]

Anti-immigrant sentiment has long been present as a powerful strand within European politics. But it has been intensified by the politics of the refugee crisis. The EU struggled to manage the massive arrival of refugees and migrants from the Middle East that began in 2015. By the end of that year over a million migrants and refugees had arrived in Europe.[21] By 2016, 5.2 million refugees and migrants had reached Europe.[22] The main driver of this mass migration was the civil war in Syria, which ravaged the country and drew the Great Powers into rival alliances with competing Syrian factions. The United States and the West backed the rebels that had challenged Bashar al-Assad's government. Russia and Iran backed the Assad regime. Isis intervened from their Iraqi heartlands as the country descended into chaos. In addition to hundreds of thousands of people arriving from Syria, the second largest countries of origin were Afghanistan and Iraq respectively.[23] This demonstrates the tight linkage between Europe's migrant and refugee crisis and the geopolitical deterioration of the Middle East since the disastrous 2001 Anglo-American interventions that sought 'regime change' in Afghanistan and Iraq.

Xenophobic nationalism has risen in all of the European countries most affected by the crisis and populist parties have been able to make electoral gains as a result. Many of the new arrivals first landed in Greece and Italy, two countries whose economies had been hit hard by the effects of the financial crisis and the Eurozone slowdown that followed. In both countries, nationalist anti-immigrant sentiment has risen. Of the over one million new asylum seekers and migrants who reached European territory in 2015, more than 850,000 of them did so by arriving in one of the Greek Aegean islands (UNHCR 2016). Political support for the extreme right-wing Golden Dawn party in the 2015 elections increased in those islands most affected by the influx.[24]

In Italy, between 2014 and 2017, well over 100,000 migrants and refugees arrived annually.[25] The massive increase in migratory inflows led to a hardening stance on immigration, which dominated debate in the run-up to the 2018 election. At the same time, the murderous rampage of the far-right sympathizer Luca Traini injured six people of sub-Saharan African origin and heightened the sense of an increasingly fraught political climate. Both of the eventual Coalition partners who won the 2018 election capitalized on the incident to rail against what Lega Nord's Matteo Salvini (now Italy's Deputy Prime Minister) described as 'uncontrolled immigration' linked to growing social conflict.[26]

Austria and Sweden also received high levels of asylum

seekers between 2015 and 2016 and witnessed a corresponding deepening of political polarization. Sweden's anti-immigration party, the Swedish Democrats, saw their share of the national vote increase, securing 49 seats in the Swedish parliament in 2014. In Austria, the anti-immigration Freedom Party gained 26 per cent of the votes in the 2017 elections. In both countries, violence against asylum seekers and refugees has increased.[27] By September 2018, the Swedish Democrats had further increased their national vote share to 17.6 per cent as anti-immigrant sentiment rose again.[28]

But the primary European destinations for the arriving migrants and refugees were Germany and Hungary. By 2016, Germany had already registered over one million people in its system for counting asylum applicants.[29] More than 200,000 further applications were made in 2017.[30] Increased immigration fuelled the rapid rise of the Eurosceptic Alternative for Germany (AfD) founded in 2013. Beginning as an almost single-issue, anti-euro party, it quickly morphed into an anti-immigrant and increasingly right-wing force to capitalize on the anxiety and discontent produced by the refugee crisis. By September 2017, the AfD had won 13 per cent of the national vote in elections based on a promise to strengthen borders and restore national pride. It became the third largest party in the Bundestag, doing so at the expense of mainstream political parties that suffered their worst results in the post-war period. Supporters of the AfD refer to the threat posed to German culture and identity by an influx of (predominantly Muslim) immigrants.[31] This theme, one of national culture and identity under siege, resonates throughout the populist nationalism sweeping through Europe.

Hungary's political reaction to the refugee crisis was more drastic, immediate, and draconian than that experienced in Germany. Viktor Orban blended hostility towards refugees and migrants with a strident EU-scepticism. Railing against the influx of the 'mostly muslim' incomers, Orban argued that Europe was in fact 'mentoring them'. He began to style himself as the embattled defender of European (white) Christianity against the refugees, who he described as law-breakers and potential terrorists welcomed into Hungary by an array of conspiratorial forces spanning from multinational capital to domestic left-wingers. Hungary's response to the refugee crisis included the establishment of a border police patrol, the construction of a large fence, and the demarcation of unpermitted crossing over the Hungarian border as a custodial offence.[32] Building on the anti-immigrant sentiment fuelled by the refugee crisis, Orban has extended his vision of a Christian Europe as a rallying call for like-minded parties in other, particularly Central and East European, states.[33] As in many other states, the anti-immigrant reaction to the refugee crisis has been blended with post-crisis EU-scepticism to solidify populist challenges to the status quo.

Explaining the right-wing tenor of populist movements within the US and UK requires some different considerations. Refugee and immigrant inflows into the UK from 2015 were more modest than for many other European countries. But despite this, immigration figured extremely prominently in the debate over Brexit. The United States barely accepted any refugees relative to its size and the country's leading role in collapsing the Middle Eastern geopolitical order. From a peak of

12,000 Syrian refugees accepted by the United States in 2016, the number had declined to around 100 by 2018 in the wake of Trump's 120-day 'refugee ban', which provoked a constitutional crisis.[34]

What, then, explains the reactionary thrust of populism in these countries? In the United States, the popularity of Trump's racist discourse against minorities is in part a reflection of the long-standing racial divisions within US politics that stretch back centuries to the days of slavery. These divisions have been mobilized politically before, most notably under President Nixon's 'Southern Strategy', which sought to use coded (and overtly) racist messages to harness the racial hostility of white voters in the southern United States towards blacks and other minorities in order to build a national Republican electoral majority.[35] The presence of a black President in the White House helped swell these long-standing undercurrents.[36] Allied to this, shifting demographics challenged the majority status of white ethnicity within the US population. US census data showed that between 2015 and 2017 America's absolute white population actually declined, for the first time ever recorded.[37] All of this is framed within a wider international context of rising Islamophobia, a product of the security response to 9/11. These dynamics have been cynically harnessed by Trump and other figures on the right to sow the toxic seeds of discord and division.[38]

In the UK, the politics of immigration were hugely important to the Brexit vote. But the sources of anxiety were different from those on the continent. British immigration anxieties were prompted by large-scale migration from the new member states of the EU (countries like Poland and Romania), alongside increased migratory flows from southern European countries like Spain and Greece that had been ravaged by the Eurozone crisis. As divergent growth rates between Britain and the Eurozone emerged from late 2012, EU immigration into Britain rose with them. As Eurozone growth stalled, Britain became (alongside Germany) the 'employer of last resort' within the EU labour market. With immigration increasingly politicized, the Conservative Party took a tougher stance on the issue, promising to hit specified net migration targets in a way that jarred with EU law on free movement.[39] The heightened salience of immigration as a political issue spurred the rise of UKIP.[40] By the time the refugee crisis struck in the summer of 2015, UKIP's Nigel Farage was able to use sensationalist images of mass refugee movements into Europe to stir pre-existing anti-immigrant sentiment. Immigration became a highly prominent issue in the Leave campaign.

National liberalism

Throughout the West, the response to the tension between globalizing markets and the domestic welfare of citizens has taken the form of a nativist reactivation of the nation state as a shield against 'outsider' threats to the body politic. Social liberalism, in the form of values of openness, tolerance, and compassion at the heart of a well-functioning liberal democracy, is now in peril. Reactionary nationalism is ascendant. But what about the economic policies promised by these new political forces and governing elites? Do they really break from the neoliberal paradigm that has governed the most recent phase of globalization? The answer to this question is not uniform across countries. There are important national variations in the economic policies espoused by ascendant right-wing forces. These variations reflect the different political cultures, institutional makeup, geographical location, and national histories of these different countries.

Nationalism has risen throughout Western politics, but the strength of economic liberalism varies depending on the position of each country within globalization. For those at the core who have been the main drivers of globalization, like the US, UK, and Germany, the commitment to economic liberalism remains strong. For those countries within the European periphery, like Hungary and Poland, nationalist strength is combined with a weakening of free-market ideas. These economic policies contain promising progressive moves towards redistribution and welfare that might help curb the excesses of globalization. But, sadly, they are paradoxically allied to a deeply regressive and toxic social agenda of exclusion and resentment.

Within the countries at the core of the globalization project, the combination of an ascendant nationalist nativism paired with the continued dominance of neoliberal economic ideas is extremely dangerous. It stirs popular resentment against the excesses of the neoliberal globalization project without fundamentally addressing the structural problems at its heart. It threatens to disappoint those mobilized in the hope of a better life and generate the foundations for more toxic and atavistic political forms to emerge. National liberalism promises national revival without addressing the core failures of contemporary globalization – denigrating migrants and refugees while failing to tackle the excesses brought about by the extension of the market through trade and capital flow liberalization.

In Europe, the post-communist countries at the periphery have broken most sharply with neoliberal orthodoxy. Shaped by their Soviet legacies, countries like Hungary and Poland have selectively repudiated the rule of the market and extended the socially protective influence of the state. Popular memories and institutional legacies of socialism in these countries have provided the intellectual basis for a greater willingness to develop anti-market views and encourage policies of enhanced social protection against market inequalities. This has led to a curious combination of right-wing social values with left-leaning economic ideas.[41] It is this socialist legacy, and the unpopularity of the rapid transition to capitalism during the 1990s, that gives the economic policy content of parties like Hungary's Fidesz and Poland's PiS their anti-market flavour.

Poland's government has introduced a popular subsidy programme for families with children and rolled back unpopular pension reforms.[42] PiS have combined their strident anti-immigrant rhetoric with an emphasis on the need to tackle inequality and promote stronger welfare policies, allowing them to build a broad basis of support.[43] The Fidesz government has extended state influence in many areas of the economy. There have been nationalizations in the banking and energy sectors as well as subsidies for mortgage and small business lending rates.[44] But alongside these changes, Orban has maintained a regressive flat income tax rate (with poorer and wealthier citizens paying the same rate) and the highest VAT rate (a tax with regressive effects) in the EU.[45]

Anti-market sentiments are also visible within populist forces in core Eurozone countries such as France. Marine Le Pen's Front National has combined strong anti-immigrant rhetoric and conservative social values with an increasingly left-wing economic agenda that challenges the free-market mantras of the European Union. The Front National has extended its nativist reassertion of national sovereignty into a proposed 'patriotic' economic model that would promote French business and protect the economy from foreign investment, freeing it from European 'constraints'. Alongside these measures the Front National has advocated a Keynesian domestic economic agenda of increased public spending, income redistribution and public services expansion.[46] But the party's challenge to the neoliberal order remains limited. It combines these statist proposals with free-market demands for the reduction of regulatory restrictions on business and removal of taxation on overtime.[47]

Within the two Anglo-American states that have been central to the globalization project, Britain and the United States, the challenge to the foundations of the neoliberal economic project has been notably muted. Neither Trump, nor the conservative forces aligned behind promoting Brexit, is interested in tackling the structural problems such as spiralling inequality, environmental degradation, and financial instability that have been produced by the neoliberal policies associated with globalization. In the United States, Trump has introduced massive corporate tax cuts, providing a major distributional boost to wealthy Americans. With regard to the promotion of liberalized financial flows, Trump has been a keen advocate of rolling back post-crisis regulations introduced to stabilize the US financial sector. In terms of environmental policy, Trump has looked to defang domestic environmental agencies and has withdrawn the United States from the Paris agreement to reduce global carbon emissions. In the UK, neoliberal forces with close links to senior pro-Leave figures in the Conservative Party are already mobilizing to promote a more extreme free-market agenda after Brexit, with a potential free trade agreement with the United States as a means of restructuring the UK's domestic economic model.[48]

Recovering a progressive (inter)nationalism

Progressive responses to the crisis of globalization are urgently needed. Alternative visions of how to organize a more just and sustainable world economy can help prevent a destructive slide into rival xenophobic nationalisms, economic stagnation, and democratic decay. These progressive alternatives need to tackle the deep structural problems of contemporary capitalism without sacrificing positive cosmopolitan social values and a commitment to international cooperation and solidarity. Rather than targeting migrants and refugees, progressive forces need to build a positive story of inclusion, in which the redistribution of resources and the curbing of market excesses enables the creation of an increasingly inclusive democratic politics.

Encouraging signs of progressive revitalization can be seen in many countries. New forces on the left have emerged and although they have yet to win office within any of the major advanced capitalist states, they are pointing the way towards a more equitable and sustainable future for the global economy. From the Syriza government in Greece, to the breakthrough of Podemos in Spain, Jeremy Corbyn's rise as the leader of Britain's Labour Party, and Bernie Sanders' powerful campaign for the Democratic presidential candidacy in the United States, progressive alternatives to neoliberal globalization are taking shape.

The rebirth of the left is taking on a distinctive generational hue. Older politicians like Corbyn and Sanders, who both pre-date and have outlasted the embrace of neoliberal policies by progressive parties, have made the initial breakthrough. They have acted as the symbolic figureheads of a resurgent left politics in the UK and US. But beneath them, parties have been opened up to a much younger and more diverse generation of new members and politicians. This demographic union of the old and the new left has managed to sidestep the obstacle posed by the centrist consensus embraced by a middle-generation of career politicians. Those career politicians had pulled social democratic parties towards the neoliberal consensus during the 1990s and early 2000s. Politicians of this ilk embraced untrammelled globalization under the leadership of figures like Tony Blair in the UK and Bill Clinton in the US, with leaders of social democratic parties across Europe following suit.

Within the heartland countries of the globalization project, the most concerted and significant break from neoliberalism has been the transformation of the Labour Party under the leadership of Jeremy Corbyn. After a shock victory in the Labour leadership campaign in September 2015, Corbyn has stabilized his authority over the party and made a radical break from the accommodation of some of the core tenets of neoliberalism that characterized Tony Blair's New Labour project. To do so, Corbyn successfully resisted internal attempts to supplant him by aggrieved centrists from the New Labour era. By 2018, party membership under Corbyn had swollen to over 550,000 – making Labour the largest political party in Europe. These efforts to reinvigorate the democratic basis of the party have been embodied by the role of Momentum, the grass-roots movement that has been tasked with advancing and defending Corbyn's agenda to transform the party.[49] Momentum has attracted controversy for its attempts to influence the structures of the party at all levels.[50] But by widening the social movement base of the party, Corbyn has reconnected Labour to more grass-roots participation and strengthened the party's appeal to a younger demographic of newly politicized voters.

These efforts at boosting democratic accountability within the party have been matched by a corresponding economic policy shift – one that has radically intensified Labour's commitment to democratizing the management of the economy. In what has been aptly described as an 'institutional turn' in its economic policy, Labour has set out a bold agenda to transform Britain's economy.[51] Focusing on ownership, control, and participation within the economy, Labour has outlined policies seeking to decentralize power and rebuild the devastated post-industrial regions that have been casualties of an economic model overridingly geared towards the prosperity of services sector workers in London and the South East.

Under Corbyn's leadership and guided by the strategic vision of Shadow Chancellor John McDonnell, Labour has advocated the renationalization of major utilities, the development of a national investment fund to target regions stricken by the uneven effects of globalization, and the creation of regionally focused industrial policy linked to regional public banks tasked with channelling capital to productive long-term economic activities.[52] It has also outlined plans to empower workers within corporate management by giving them a stake of ten per cent in large companies. Any company with more than 250 employees would be required to transfer shares to an 'inclusive ownership fund' controlled by the company's workers. At least one per cent of ownership would be transferred into the fund each year, up to a maximum of ten per cent.[53] Policies like these provide a route to tackling the deep structural problems that have developed within neoliberal globalization. They open space for a more equitable and democratic economic model that can enfranchise citizens and workers in a more fundamental sense, moving beyond the crisis of representative government by creating deeper overlapping structures of regional and workplace democracy. Deepening and widening democratic engagement can sap the support base of reactionary demagogues by meaningfully reconnecting people to the governance of their workplaces and communities.

In the United States, a more nascent but comparable transformation is underway within the Democratic Party. Bernie Sanders' ideas have challenged neoliberal orthodoxy within the party and reinvigorated a younger generation of voters and politicians. Sanders shot to prominence with his bid for the Democratic candidacy in the 2016 presidential election. Despite ultimately losing out to Hillary Clinton in the primaries, Sanders' unorthodox and socialist policy platform resonated deeply with a new generation of American voters. His campaign broke the stranglehold of neoliberal policies on the public debate around economic policy.

Outlining a transformative agenda for the American economy, Sanders has called for universal government-provided health insurance, free college tuition, a near-doubling of the minimum wage to $15 per hour, stronger trade union rights, and higher taxes on the wealthy. Targeting the staggering levels of wealth and income inequality within the United States, Sanders has been outspoken and uncompromising in his attacks on the 'billionaire class'. He has called for an additional $1.6 trillion per year in taxes, with 40 per cent of those extra taxes to be levied from households in the top one per cent of income earners – those with annual incomes over $500,000.[54] These arguments around raising the top rate of tax are starting to shift the debate in the United States, with the influential economist Paul Krugman endorsing calls for a higher top tax rate in a recent column for the *New York Times*.[55]

Sanders' unexpected success has paved the way for a wider transformation of the Democratic Party. A new generation of ethnically diverse, young, and increasingly female candidates are pulling the party to the left. After the most recent mid-term elections, in which the Democrats made significant gains, 37 per cent of Democrats in Congress are people of colour – making the representation much closer to the actual ethnic makeup of America. Added to this, there are now three times as many elected Democratic women as there are Republican women in Congress.[56]

The changing face of the Democratic Party, and of American progressive politics more broadly, is embodied by Senator Alexandria Ocasio-Cortez. A 29-year-old woman of Puerto Rican descent who comes from the Bronx and describes herself as a democratic socialist, having previously worked for Sanders' campaign team, Ocasio-Cortez stormed to victory in the mid-term Congressional elections. She became the youngest woman ever to be elected to Congress with an overwhelming majority of votes in the Fourteenth District of New York.[57] Ocasio-Cortez has echoed the radicalism of Sanders by calling for universal healthcare, cancellation of student debts and provision of tuition-free college education, a universal jobs guarantee, and a human right to housing, campaign finance reform, the transformation of immigration policy and a 'Green New Deal' to tackle climate change.[58]

What first appeared as a radical rupture from existing policies with Sanders' shock appeal in 2016 has now become a more standard position within the party. Sanders' progressive competitor for the 2020 Presidential campaign – Massachusetts Senator Elizabeth Warren – is also promoting a wide-ranging reform agenda. She has called for aggressive anti-corruption legislation, challenged corporate trade deals that have lowered US wages, and demanded worker representation on the boards of large corporations that echoes the policy proposed by the UK Labour Party.[59] If politicians like Sanders, Ocasio-Cortez, and Warren can continue to propel a thorough departure from neoliberalism within the Democratic Party, Americans may be presented with a strong progressive alternative to Trump's reactionary national liberalism in 2020.

Important breakthroughs for the left have also occurred across continental Europe. Jean-Luc Mélenchon's newly formed left-wing alliance 'La France

Insoumise' (Unbowed France) captured almost 20 per cent of the popular vote in the first round of France's 2017 election, while support for the Socialist Party collapsed. Mélenchon has subjected the neoliberal policy thrust of the EU to searing critique, calling for a rejection of austerity policies through major increases in public spending and higher tax rates for the very wealthy. In an interesting parallel with the UK and US contexts, Mélenchon was far ahead of his contenders when it came to the youth vote, capturing 30 per cent of the vote among 18 to 24-year-olds.[60]

The most impressive electoral breakthrough for the left in the years since the financial crisis has occurred in Greece, with the election of the Syriza government to power in 2015 during the peak of the austerity crisis in Greece. Syriza had emerged as a broad left-wing coalition through its support for protests, occupations and strikes in Greece from 2011 onwards. The coalition of interests was formally announced as a single political party in 2013. One of the strengths of Syriza was its ability to galvanize a broader base of popular support beyond the Greek parliament, widening its democratic basis through its close links to social movements that had developed in response to the drastic austerity measures implemented by the so-called 'Troika' of the European Commission, European Central Bank, and International Monetary Fund in return for emergency bailout funds from 2010 as the sovereign debt crisis in Europe crashed the Greek economy.[61]

Despite Syriza's success in breaking the grip of the discredited agenda of the social democratic PASOK party, the project to transform the Greek economy and society ultimately fell apart under the pressure of extreme fiscal strain and the political power of the Troika. The Troika proved unwilling to negotiate with Syriza. And ultimately, Syriza proved unwilling to countenance the kind of rupture from the euro and the European Union that would have been required to reset Greece's economic trajectory. Such a move, involving a chaotic reintroduction of the drachma without the financial support of the EU, would have inflicted even deeper suffering on the Greek population. But it would also have enabled a longer-term transition to greater fiscal and monetary autonomy. Regaining autonomy would likely have come at far too high a cost.

The Greek experience neatly captures the dilemma that those seeking to escape the constraints of neoliberal globalization face – the extreme pro-market emphasis of contemporary globalization and the restrictive rules that tie the hands of governments under the type of deep economic integration exemplified by the EU are in tension with democratic projects to restore economic autonomy. But the costs of exiting deeper forms of integration are so high that, particularly for smaller economies, they threaten to undermine the social and economic basis for a more progressive economic vision. Allowing more space for national governments to implement progressive economic policies, from taxation to trade and public spending, will require a more flexible set of rules governing globalization. It will also require rules that are written more in the interests of workers and democratic governments and less in the interests of large transnational corporations. Developing countries also need to benefit more from international trade arrangements, raising working conditions and living standards in these countries.

What might this reformed vision of globalization look like? Existing trade deals have emphasized free capital mobility and enabled corporations to shift investment and jobs to countries with lower wages, weaker labour standards, and more permissive environmental regulations. Instead, trade deals should guarantee strict standards of corporate accountability and empower workers employed by MNCs whatever country they are employed in. The emphasis on free trade should be replaced by a commitment to fairer trade – ensuring that increased levels of international trade and investment benefit workers and help contribute to raising labour and environmental standards globally. Raising labour standards and increasing wages can help reduce global inequality by increasing the share of income that goes to workers globally (reducing corporate super-profits). In terms of the legal enforcement of contemporary trade deals, courts should not focus on the prerogative of companies to sue national governments for loss of profits (the premise of Investor State Dispute Settlement courts that were proposed within the Trans-Pacific Partnership). They should instead allow citizens, trade unions and other groups from within civil society to hold corporations to account for labour conditions and environmental standards.[62]

Trade deals also need to give national governments much more leeway to promote national and local firms in the interest of dealing with climate change and enabling regional regeneration for the areas worst affected by the inequities of globalization. This may of course ultimately mean a reduced level of world trade in some areas that are particularly environmentally significant. And it will mean enabling governments to regulate flows of international investment by prioritizing green domestic industries and closing out foreign corporations when their business strategies are not considered to be compatible with national economic, social, and environmental development. But a globalization that allows more democratic flexibility will also help reset the world economy on a more economically, politically, and environmentally sustainable basis.

Permitting more democratic autonomy on issues of trade and investment will allow progressive governments to address some of the deep structural problems of the contemporary global economy, without sacrificing the broader commitment to openness and integration. It will also foster a much more welcoming and positive context for both economic migrants and refugees. The temptation to hide behind militarized border walls and increasingly stringent ideas of citizenship should be avoided. Migration needs to be invested in and harnessed for the development of a new economic settlement within countries so that new arrivals cannot easily be represented as a drain on scarce public resources. Making political and economic institutions at the national and local level more democratic, while raising the wage share of national income through stronger unionization and higher minimum wages, can enable a more inclusive and positive environment for migrants and refugees. There is no necessity for economic migration to undercut the wages of domestic workers if the regulatory and legal conditions for employment are effectively designed and enforced.

These national efforts should also be buttressed by multilateral funding, in particular for climate refugees, so that countries affected by increased refugee flows can receive financial support from wealthier countries that have disproportionately generated the climate change and geopolitical instability driving refugee flows. Progressive movements and parties throughout the world will need to work towards a global framework for the twenty-first century that enables more democratic autonomy and offers a more progressive settlement for those countries that support economic interdependence.

A bold progressive agenda may seem wildly utopian, even quixotic. But it can be helped by the presence of a unifying challenge that prompts countries to re-evaluate the foundations of their economic and social models. Climate change represents exactly this kind of challenge. But there is, of course, no inevitability in its promise to open up and motivate progressive alternatives to neoliberal globalization. At present the failure to adequately respond to climate change looks more likely to unleash the forces of barbarism than to rally the forces of progress. Shaping the connection between the domestic and global responses to climate change in a cooperative and mutually supportive way will be critical to ensuring a positive future for the world economy.

5

Planning for the Anthropocene

Saving the global economy from the spectre of disintegration will not be easy. The extraordinary breadth and depth of contemporary globalization buys us time. But the more pervasive condition of globalization has also, paradoxically, dramatically increased the challenge of making the world economy sustainable. The current crisis of globalization is unique because, unlike the global crises of the past, the traditional fix of expanded carbon-intensive economic growth can no longer resolve the tensions between global markets and national politics. The requirement of greater political and economic sustainability for globalization is now bound up with the planetary peril of climate change.

The travails of globalization are now overlaid upon a much deeper historical crisis of human civilization. The fossil fuel energy sources that have underpinned the spectacular growth of human population and material prosperity since the eighteenth century are running out. Not only are they running out, their continued use has now reached (and perhaps breached) the natural limits imposed by the earth's climate. Centuries of rising carbon emissions and human expansion into ever wider reaches of the earth's ecosystem have heralded the arrival of the 'Anthropocene' – a new geological epoch in which humanity itself is now the major driver of climatic and earth systems transformation. Continued carbon emissions associated with fossil fuel usage and global economic growth threaten to bring about dangerous and unpredictable transformations to the earth's climate.[1]

In the Anthropocene age, saving globalization can only be achieved through a wholesale transformation of the form, content, and purpose of global economic interdependence. A transformation that unites the goals of enhanced political and economic wellbeing with ecological stability in a way that has not previously been achieved. Any attempt to deal with the failures and injustices of neoliberal globalization, from financial instability to inequality, will need to be part of a broader ecological strategy to render human life on earth compatible with environmental stability. Reconciling global economic interdependence with national sovereignty and popular political consent is now only one dimension of a broader challenge of reconciling human society with planetary vitality.

Politics under the Anthropocene is not, though, an exclusively negative project. It presents new opportunities alongside the new constraints. The planetary challenge of averting ecological catastrophe has the potential to act as a unique rallying call for global solidarity and cooperation. It can act as a tonic to the temptations of nationalist disintegration. The policy puzzles surrounding economic growth and sustainability posed by the Anthropocene should form the basis for a new consensus required to reconfigure the global economy by tackling issues of inequality, democratic accountability, and environmental sustainability.

Adapting to the Anthropocene will involve moving beyond the free-market doctrine of neoliberalism. Indeed, this may prove to be the end of the road for the ambitious liberal visions of political economy set in motion from the late eighteenth century. Markets alone have so far proved inadequate to dealing with the problems posed by climate change. The logic of unlimited economic growth that underpins capitalism may well be irreconcilable with the goal of stabilizing our environment. Curbing our consumption and using renewable resources in a more environmentally friendly way requires a new vision of a decentralized, coordinating state that intervenes through democratic planning to sustainably shape national development within a wider rules-based international order. But this does not mean the end of globalization. While certain forms of globalized interconnectedness such as volatile short-term capital flows, environmentally unsustainable consumption patterns, trade and production will need to be scaled back, other forms of global cooperation and solidarity will need to be enhanced to meet the challenges of the Anthropocene.

Western countries may need to look both historically to their past, and geographically towards the East, to see the outlines of a different political economy. Thinking historically can allow us to learn from the successes, while also acknowledging the failures, of the more state-directed and planned post-Second World War mixed economy in the West. We should not forget that this was an economic model associated with a period of unprecedented economic equality and democratic energy. Expanding our geographical horizons by looking towards Asia for inspiration can help us recognize that China's success, and that of other East Asian economies before it, demonstrates the tremendous power of the state and strategic planning geared towards longer-term goals of economic and social development. Learning from these examples can provide clues as to how to navigate the unprecedented challenges of the Anthropocene.

Towards a green developmental state

The most egalitarian and democratically legitimate period of the globalization project coincided with the 'embedded liberalism' that governed the international economy after the Second World War. Under this settlement, the commitment to freer international trade and finance was balanced with a recognition of the importance of domestic economic and social welfare and full employment. Higher top income and corporate tax rates ensured a more equal distribution of national wealth and wages increased in step with rising economic productivity. Controls on the free movement of capital insulated governments from the speculative pressures of investors and enabled stable exchange rates alongside a high level of autonomy for domestic economic policy. Living standards improved and a period of unprecedentedly high economic growth rates followed. Of course, the benefits of the embedded liberal settlement did not reach all parts of the world equally. Many countries in the Global South continued to play the role of subordinate raw material suppliers to the rapidly growing advanced economies. Politically, Western powers continued to intervene in the affairs of developing countries, in violation of their sovereignty and autonomy.

One of the main ingredients in the success of post-war economic development was the expanded role of the state within the management of the economy. The rise of Keynesian strategies for managing economic performance enabled a compromise between the polarized strategies of central planning and laissez-faire. Keynes sought to balance greater strategic control over economic performance with a continued commitment to market freedom. In practical terms, this meant that the government would intervene by determining the overall level of economic output, but not the content or methods of economic production. The intervention Keynes envisaged was indirect, altering market choices by adjusting the level of government spending and taxation. It was to be implemented by a technocratic elite of civil servants who would be insulated from democratic pressures.[2]

In some Western economies the methods of government intervention went beyond the indirect and technocratic approach that Keynes had advocated. Economic planning of a more direct kind was introduced. Governments accepted that the state should intervene to promote particular areas of production with the understanding that specific sectors would be more beneficial to the overall development of the economy. In France, planning was geared towards the strategic development of sectors that were seen as central to the wider national economic model. French planners also sought to achieve specific social objectives, working towards the goal of a 'more complete view of man' in the Fourth Plan implemented between 1962 and 1965.[3] A central planning agency staffed with elite bureaucrats was used to grow industry, while government-owned firms played a central role in propelling economic growth.[4]

The challenges of economic depression and war on a massive scale drove the enlarged state capacity that informed Keynesian economic management and the broader turn to planning. The two world wars acted as a catalyst for the transformation of the modern state. They expanded its administrative capacities and command over resources. Markets and private business on their own were not able to bring about the unifying strategic vision or coordination of economic activity required to prepare for war. War-time price controls and production loosened the market's grip on the control of national assets, finance, and production as the state steered economic activity towards military mobilization. Techniques of economic planning began to hold sway.

There is an important parallel here with the challenge of the Anthropocene. The state is the most important and enduring institution of human political and economic organization. Just as the state was transformed in the face of the problems posed by economic depression and industrialized total war, it will now have to be reimagined and repurposed to meet a new set of challenges as the threat of climate change deepens.

It is not only to the history of post-war Western economic development that we should look to find the merits of a less market-dependent and more interventionist approach. From the 1950s to the 1980s, a number of East Asian economies experienced rapid development based on a more strategic and expanded role for the state. Countries like Japan, Taiwan, and South Korea experienced rapid development by gearing the state towards a strategic relationship with economic development. Close linkages between government officials and private business enabled the gearing of development towards targeted sectors. This model provided high job security and a long-term approach to investment decisions.[5]

Some East Asian economies went further than others in limiting the scope of market authority over economic policy. Japan became the template for the approach, but it was in South Korea that the market was shaped most extensively by the influence of the state. An extremely powerful South Korean government agency propelled an industrial policy that restricted market control over economic decision-making. These policies were implemented through a banking sector under public ownership, enabling credit to be targeted at strategic sectors and reducing the influence of private capital markets over economic policy.[6] Five-year plans were used to guide the coordination of economic policy. Financial flows within the country, and the movement of capital across Korean borders, were both tightly controlled.[7]

The regulation of trade and financial liberalization was an important part of the East Asian development 'miracle'. It spurred rapid growth and rising living standards. Trade liberalization was adopted only in a gradual and constrained way. Governments recognized the importance of building up and maintaining the export capacity of domestic firms. Even if that meant sheltering them from international competition. The market was also restricted when it came to industrial production. Governments in Taiwan, South Korea, and Japan created returns that were above market rates to encourage greater investment into the sectors that had been prioritized. Political coalitions, between the governing party and private business, were formed to stabilize these linkages over time. High levels of domestic savings were funnelled into productive investment.[8]

East Asian approaches to rapid economic catch-up with the West came to be known as the 'developmental state'. The concept was premised on the idea that the state could build up its political legitimacy and popular support by improving economic performance through the use of a selective industrial policy. Reviving the idea of the developmental state is one way of dealing with the challenges of the Anthropocene and the sustained market failures, ranging from inadequate supply of housing to financial instability, that have characterized globalization in the neoliberal era.

But a developmental state for the Anthropocene also has to be different. It needs to retain the market-curbing impetus of industrial policy and financial regulation, alongside an improved capability for the state to manage economic development strategically over the medium and long term. But it also needs to place *green policies*, not the pursuit of unfettered growth, at the core of its quest for enhanced political legitimacy and popular consent.

This, then, has to be a transformation in both the *means* and the *ends* of the state. Two big changes need to happen. Firstly, unbridled growth encapsulated by the universal goal of boosting GDP can no longer stand at the heart of our understanding of what economic development is. And secondly, a green developmental state needs to be more democratic and more decentralized if it is to plug the legitimacy gap that blights contemporary Western politics and threatens globalization.

Repurposing the state to deal with climate change cannot involve a simple return to the dominance of technocratic, centralized, state administrators. The need to revive democracy and tackle the regional disparities of wealth generated by globalization requires a more decentralized and participatory form of planning in the age of the Anthropocene. Of course, economies of scale mean that some large green infrastructure projects will need to be centrally funded and administered. But wherever possible, funding and direction of green economic transformation should be devolved to the highest possible degree. This will enable the urgent needs for democratic renewal, progressive redistribution, and green economic transformation to be met together within a broad vision of social change. In 2018, major international cities and states met in San Francisco to create their own Paris-style agreement, with California (the world's fifth largest economy) pledging to be carbon neutral by 2045. New York City has committed to divesting its vast pension fund from fossil fuel investments.[9] Leadership from major cities will not be enough on its own, but it can help give momentum and credibility to tackling climate change.

Planning for the Anthropocene must look different from previous strategies of economic and social development. Economic growth, for so long the centrepiece of all development strategies, will have to be radically transformed. Either it will have to be rendered much more sustainable, by shifting away from carbon-intensive production processes and consumption habits and towards renewable sources of energy. Or the very notion of economic growth itself may even have to be downgraded from its current position as the main goal of economic development. We will have to think of broader understandings of human welfare and progress that can guide our economic development.[10]

Clues to what a green developmental state might look like are not to be found only in the past. Contemporary Chinese development provides an important example both of the value of a long-term strategic state influence over economic policy *and* the importance of finding more environmentally sustainable ways of promoting economic development. And it matters because China's approach to dealing with climate change, alongside that of India, the United States and the EU, will be hugely important to the future of our planet. Since the late 1970s, economic reform in China has brought about the emergence of a distinctive pathway towards economic development. The Chinese approach to economic development and modernization has involved a strong role for state control over key sectors, notably the banking sector. Long-term national development goals are placed at the centre of economic policy and specific sectors are targeted for promotion. Just as with the earlier examples of East Asian development, the opening up to global competition in terms of trade and finance has been controlled and gradual.

Unlike earlier examples of East Asian state-led development, though, China has relied upon powerful local state agencies that connect national development to diverse regional strategies.[11] Deng Xiaoping's reformist measures from 1979 onwards strengthened existing local policy autonomy within China. Local policy-makers were empowered to develop distinctive strategies for encouraging foreign investment and building up business capacity. This more federal approach to economic development, in which different jurisdictions competed to attract investment capital, was paired with an overarching central state vision, with state-owned firms and state-sponsored research used to support long-term and higher risk economic ventures.[12] At the heart of the Chinese approach to economic development is this sometimes uneasy, but also highly dynamic, combination of top-down state-led development with decentralized local networks of policy and business elites developing economic strategies on the ground.

One of the major down-sides of China's economic development has been its disastrous environmental effects. With breakneck industrialization and growth came a massive surge in carbon dioxide emissions. China quickly became the world's top carbon dioxide emitter. China's poor air quality is such a severe health issue that it has been estimated to contribute towards 1.6 million deaths per year in the country. Thick smog hovers over the northern industrial provinces, choking the air. Pollution in China has become a major environmental and political issue. This has prompted Chinese elites to take climate change much more seriously.[13]

A number of major policy measures have been introduced to tackle environmental problems. China is now the world leader in electric car production, and it is spending more than twice as much as the United States on investment in clean-energy sources. It produces two-thirds of solar panels globally. The way that China is tackling climate change reflects the way that it goes about managing economic development. China is using its state-controlled financial sector to funnel credit into green economic initiatives. In 2012, the Chinese Banking Regulatory Commission strengthened its environmental framework through 'Green Credit Guidelines' that push banks to increase their financial support for green, low-carbon economic sectors. China is now the first country to have established official rules for environmentally friendly 'green bonds' and has become the world's largest market for them. The capacity of the Chinese state to plan its financial development has meant that green finance has rapidly been promoted as a mechanism to promote sustainable growth.[14]

We certainly should not hold up the Chinese model as an unqualified success. China's breakneck industrialization has been environmentally disastrous. Current policy measures to tackle climate change may be a case of too little too late. And it is certainly not clear that China's 'resource safari' across the African continent will offer environmental sustainability in those regions targeted by Chinese investment as sources of essential raw materials inputs for continued Chinese growth. While China's ambitious 'Belt and Road Initiative', that will bring massive investment to over 70 countries (accounting for two thirds of the world's population) sweeping from East Asia into Central Europe, could well bring with it a damaging reliance upon fossil fuels, that is if these countries try to replicate the Chinese path to rapid economic growth. Despite the cap on coal consumption within China, Chinese coal and energy companies have been expanding rapidly abroad, with Chinese coal companies involved in at least 240 coal projects in 25 Belt and Road countries.[15] And, of course, China's increasingly authoritarian approach under Xi Jinping is deeply undesirable and any policy borrowing from the Chinese example needs to be adapted to a democratic setting.

China's domestic embrace of green finance and its support for a number of forward-looking environmental policies does, though, contrast sharply with the approach taken by the United States under the leadership of President Trump. Trump has committed to rolling back a wide range of Obama-era environmental policies. These moves will hinder progress on reducing air pollution and greenhouse gases. Trump's administration is blocking the transition away from coal burning, cutting limits on the methane gas produced by oil producers and preventing policies to make new cars more environmentally friendly.[16]

The Environmental Protection Agency has been at the centre of many of these shifts away from green policies. Trump promised to disband the agency during his election campaign and followed through on this by shrinking the agency's workforce by eight per cent (the lowest since the Reagan years).[17] His appointment of Scott Pruitt, a former Oklahoma Attorney General and close ally of oil and gas companies, to head the agency signalled his intent. Pruitt went about unpicking environmental policy and encouraged Trump to withdraw from the Paris Agreement on climate change.[18] The United States announced its landmark renunciation of global attempts to combat climate change in June 2017. At the state level, divisions have emerged between Democratic states seeking to enhance environmental policies and Republican states looking to achieve the reverse. All but one of the most carbon-intensive states in the United States voted for Trump in 2016.[19] Divisions between major Democratic states like California and Trump's administration reduce the ability of the United States to provide strong and concerted leadership within global environmental policy.

Looking back to historical examples of planned economic development shows us the merits of using the strategic power of the state to bring about rapid transformation towards pre-determined goals. In the West the continued grip of free-market doctrine is a dangerous obstacle to the holistic and far-reaching transformation required to tackle climate change immediately. The dominant tendency of deregulating markets that has characterized the neoliberal era is at odds with the need for enhanced environmental regulation and planning required to meet the challenges of climate change. Free-market ideas delegitimize the positive role of government in our economic life and make it much harder to advance an agenda of redistribution, public investment, and state involvement in transitioning to a green economy.[20]

There are some encouraging signs that progressive politicians throughout the West are beginning to recognize their responsibility to lead the transition to a greener global economy. In the United States, the 'Green New Deal' is gaining increasing traction and looks likely to be a core policy issue for the Democrats going into the 2020 Presidential election. Drawing on the evocative language of Roosevelt's historical Depression-busting New Deal of the 1930s, the plan seeks to provide a massive green stimulus to the economy – creating millions of new jobs through an ambitious green economic transition ranging from a shift to carbon-neutral energy provision through the installation of solar panels, to the development of a greener industrial strategy and the manufacture of electric vehicles. These changes are geared towards meeting the Paris Agreement's commitment to prevent the earth's climate from warming by more than 2.7 degrees by 2100.[21] In the UK, the Labour Party has committed to a 'green jobs revolution' – with plans to create 400,000 skilled jobs by investing in renewable energy sources like wind and solar power, while upgrading energy efficiency of existing homes and businesses. It is hoped that 85 per cent of the country's energy needs would be met from renewable sources by 2030.[22] Pledging to be the greenest government ever, Labour has recognized that market solutions will not be adequate to tackle climate change with the scale and immediacy that is required. Planning and coordination by public authorities will play a vital role.[23]

Efforts by national governments will be critical to dealing with climate change but combining these with local initiatives can offer a more community-based and democratic response. A good example of this is the new model of worker and community-controlled enterprises being developed in the city of Cleveland in the United States. The city has been wracked by poverty and deindustrialization, but from the ruins of industrial decay a new approach to organizing the economy has begun to emerge. Employee-owned and controlled businesses with green environmental practices, like the Evergreen Cooperative Laundry, have been set up. Employees are able to gradually build up equity in the company through payroll deductions. These small-scale community business initiatives have received support from banks and the municipal government.[24]

Similar efforts have been underway in the UK too, with the Preston council in the north of England developing a bold new approach to growing the local economy. Their project of community wealth-building has involved encouraging local institutions to buy more of their goods and services from local producers – keeping money in the local economy. Additionally, the council have developed plans to generate new cooperative models of ownership within the city, drawing on the example of success in Cleveland and the business practices of the large Spanish coop – Mondragon. These examples demonstrate the ability of local, community-based initiatives to coordinate environmentally sustainable and democratically empowering responses to the economic and social malaise that has afflicted many cities and regions under contemporary globalization. This will inevitably involve less international trade and investment in certain contexts – with a greater emphasis on local-level community initiatives and wealth-building. But these initiatives need to be overlaid with international trade and investment rather than being ranged as polarized alternatives. A more varied set of economic organizations and practices at different scales can help give the flexibility needed to generate a more sustainable global economy.

At whichever levels we tackle climate change, abandoning our faith in the omnipotence of markets is crucial to meeting the challenge. There is no compelling case to be made that the market has brought us anywhere close to dealing with these challenges with the scale and scope of change required. The introduction of carbon trading since the 1990s hasn't brought about anything close to the required level of reduction in greenhouse gas emissions.[25] The global fossil fuel industry needs to be shrunk massively and rapidly to reduce emissions. Producing and consuming energy from fossil fuels is responsible for generating about 70 per cent of greenhouse gas emissions causing climate change.[26] Radically curbing fossil fuel use appears deeply unlikely if it is left to the direction of the major fossil fuel firms acting in the interests of their shareholders. Dealing with climate change will mean reducing profits in certain sectors or abandoning them altogether. It will also require massive investment – the IPPC estimates that limiting global warming to the 1.5 per cent increase agreed in Paris will require annual energy-related mitigation investment of $900 billion between 2015 and 2050.[27] This is clearly an enormous amount. Harnessing the capital involved to achieve this will require more than just new financial innovations such as green bonds. It should also be seen as an opportunity to tackle inequality by implementing progressive taxes to fund the shift to greener energy sources and unlock new green jobs. Plans for a green New Deal are an encouraging move in the right direction, but projects for green economic transformation need to connect with the communities that have been most affected by the inequalities of contemporary globalization. Many of these initiatives will have to be undertaken at the national, regional, and local levels. These strategies also need to be connected to a wider global framework.

Globalizing solidarity

One of the tragedies of climate change is its vastly uneven impact across the richer and poorer countries of the world. Despite their much more pronounced role in producing and benefiting from the fossil fuel usage and consumption that have spurred climate change, the rich countries of the Global North will actually be less acutely affected than the poorer developing countries in the Global South. The countries of the Global South, having been far less responsible for the greenhouse gas emissions causing global warming, will bear most of the brunt of the impact of rising sea levels, droughts, food shortages, and general environmental degradation.[28] The most unsustainable levels of consumption have historically been, and continue to be, located within the rich countries of the Global North. If everyone on earth consumed as much as the average American, for example, we would require six planets to support human society. If everyone on earth consumed as much as the average French person, we would still require three planets.[29] The ecological footprint of human life, understood as the total area in hectares of average biologically productive land required to support each person's lifestyle, is heavily uneven in terms of its geographical spread.

Global governance efforts at solving climate change need to have a recognition of the historical and contemporary injustices associated with climate change at their core. It is clear that the burden of adjustment should fall more heavily on the advanced economies of the West and wealthy Asian economies like Japan and South Korea. This cannot be a global policy solution in which everyone mutually benefits to an equal degree – although all societies can benefit from a transition to greener forms of economic development and social aspirations that move beyond the logic of ever-increasing consumption and growth, dealing with climate change must involve the advanced economies bearing higher costs of adjustment than the poorer countries of the developing South. It must involve, in other words, a net transfer of wealth from the countries of the North to those of the South, in an effort to assist poorer countries access the capital and expertise needed to transform the environmental basis of their economies and brace themselves for the economic, societal, and political disruption caused by greater climate instability.

Achieving global action to deal with climate change will require a greater commitment to values of international solidarity and mutual aid. It will also require us to rethink our approach to international trade and international capital flows. Trade agreements need to enable more flexibility for communities dealing with climate change and responding to economic deprivation. In the past, WTO rules have prevented the kind of buy-local and hire-local provisions involved in generating regional response to the structural problems of globalization.[30] Trade openness will need to be compromised in the interests of specific environmental and local economic regeneration goals. This kind of green protectionism needs to be accepted and embraced as part of global initiatives agreed by nation states to respond to climate change. A more managed approach to trade and capital flows is required. Cross-border capital flows into carbon-intensive and environmentally damaging sectors should be subject to highly punitive tax rates. Implementing substantial taxes on short-term capital flows would provide increased government revenue for dealing with climate change. So too would a concerted effort to clamp down on offshore tax havens, alongside the introduction of much higher top rates of tax on wealth and income. Undoubtedly, the most powerful economic and political players, the United States, China, and the European Union, will have to be at the heart of these global efforts. At a time when the most ambitious forms of international cooperation and solidarity are required, the United States' disavowal of the rules-based international order could not be more inauspiciously timed. China's growing commitment to dealing with climate change holds more promise. But as we have seen, China's approach is inconsistent, and its support for fossil-fuel usage to promote international expansion through the Belt and Road is in deep contradiction with its domestic commitment to greener development. And in a country that is increasingly authoritarian, it is not easy to see how new international policy commitments can achieve the deep domestic legitimacy required to maintain cooperation in the face of what will undoubtedly prove to be increasing stresses and strains prompted by climatic deterioration.

The lesson to be taken from this is that finding the right balance of values and commitments at the international level will only be feasible if domestic politics in the major states of the global economy can be realigned. The virtues of solidarity and justice at the international level need to be a mirror image of the dominant political trends and institutional outlooks *within* countries. Just as the historical story of the globalization project has involved various attempts to fit together domestic political commitments and international economic priorities, so too will the response to the unique challenges of the Anthropocene require us to realign our domestic politics and institutions so that they support, rather than undercut, the global solidarity that is urgently required. A green global order can only prosper if it reflects a multitude of green societies working together.

6

Global futures

Each year business elites and political leaders from around the world gather at the World Economic Forum at Davos. At this meeting perched high in the Swiss Alps, the 'Davos set' of high net worth individuals, powerful politicians, and corporate CEOs descend on mass in private jets to prognosticate about the future of the global economy. Davos has come to symbolize the commanding heights of the neoliberal globalization project. The keynote speech in January 2019 was made by the newly elected Brazilian President, Jair Bolsonaro. Bolsonaro promised an ambitious agenda to open up the Brazilian economy to foreign investment and international trade. His pro-business speech chimed with the usual tone of Davos meetings. But Bolsonaro is not your average pro-globalization politician. He is a fascist. He has promised to give the Brazilian police 'carte blanche to kill' and to strip away human rights.[1] He fondly recalls Brazil's own brutal military dictatorship and has expressed his admiration for other Latin American dictators (such as Chile's Augusto Pinochet) while denigrating ethnic minorities, ideological opponents, and the LGBT community.[2]

This unholy union between Davos and Bolsonaro demonstrates the changing character of the globalization project and the deep political crisis that its more aggressive phase has brought about. Bolsonaro's invitation to Davos and the address that he delivered embody the rising national liberalism threatening to gain control of the globalization project. If it is successful then it will only deepen inequality, weaken democracy, and drive the world ever closer towards ecological catastrophe. It is a deeply disturbing alignment between a pro-market and inegalitarian economic policy that fails to address the major problems at the heart of globalization and an increasingly authoritarian, intolerant, and xenophobic political project that whips up popular resentment against vulnerable groups within society. The receptiveness of business elites to Bolsonaro's presence at Davos suggests that the stewards of neoliberal globalization are willing to compromise on social and political liberalism in the interests of maintaining their economic freedoms.

But do the rise of national liberalism and the deep malaise of the world economy represent the end of globalization? This book has argued that they do not. They represent a more acute but hugely consequential crisis of the neoliberal phase of globalization. That crisis does, if left unchecked, have the capacity to break apart the world economy and summon an even darker shade of politics into existence. If national liberalism continues to gain momentum, then the longer-term trajectory of a peacefully interconnected world economy will be gravely imperilled. But the depth and breadth of the contemporary globalized condition raises the costs of disintegration and buys some time to build progressive alternatives to neoliberalism. It means that a return to a

1930s-style scenario of economic autarky and rivalrous militarism is highly unlikely. Today's world economy is much more deeply integrated than it was then and the constraints that prevent its breakup are much stronger.

The instability currently surrounding the global economy is the product of a deeper antinomy within the globalization project. Throughout its history, globalization has been marked by a long-standing tension between ambitious liberal visions for how to organize an integrated world economy, on the one hand, and the continued existence of distinctive nation states with their own sovereign authority, on the other. With each successive liberal vision of globalization there has been a gradual deepening of the globalized condition. But the utopianism of the liberal vision of political economy, grounded in the false promise of a separation between politics and economics, has meant that there is a gap between each different liberal vision of how to organize the global economy, understood as an ideal, and the practical workings of each era of globalization. Politics, power, hierarchy, and inequality always get in the way of the realization of the liberal vision of self-regulating international markets beyond politics. In the age of the Anthropocene, the fundamental liberal promise of unending economic growth based on the use of the earth's resources has now also been called into question.

As I have argued in this book, thinking about the current crisis of globalization in a more historical way can help us diagnose more precisely the problems that we are facing. It can also help us to think more clearly about what needs to be done to overcome them. It reveals the long-standing tensions within the liberal economic vision for how to organize a world of differ-ent nation states through a system of trade and financial flows. Some of these liberal visions have delivered better results than others, but ultimately, they have all proved unsuccessful in creating an enduring and sustainable basis for how to organize the global economy. The longer history of globalization shows us that we cannot create a foolproof design for a global economic system removed from politics and democracy. Nor should we want to. Instead, we need to recognize that visions of the international economy need to be flexible enough to accommodate the changing priorities of domestic politics.

We can learn some positive lessons from thinking his-torically about globalization, but there are also pitfalls to avoid when thinking historically too. Descending into hyperbolic comparisons with the 1930s will not help us understand the specific challenges faced by today's world economy. Comparisons with the 1930s are more likely to generate a mood of despair and defeatism, rather than generating the kind of democratic political energy and momentum required to propel progressive political and economic solutions. The conditions that brought the world economy into ruinous confrontation then were unique. They reflected the flimsier foundations of a much less well-established international economic system and a more nascent era of globalization when compared to now. In our more interdependent world economy of today, with colonial imperialism no longer a viable strategy of international economic policy, most countries have little alternative but to continue support-ing the cross-border flows of goods and capital that sustain their economies within a much more complex and far-reaching international division of labour. And with the existence of nuclear weapons and other instruments of modern warfare that drastically raise the cost of conflict, a slide into rampant militarism between the world's great powers is much less likely.

If we are to compare our troubled times to a previous historical epoch it is to the crisis of the 1970s that we should look. The capacity of the international economy to survive the strains of the 1970s without collapse shows that although the challenges today are deep and grave, there are still strong forces binding the global economy together and making a total disintegration less likely. Making the right historical comparisons with previous crises of globalization helps us put current events into perspective. It allows us to avoid sensationalist thinking about the collapse of the world economy that clouds our judgement and makes it harder to see positive ways out of our current predicament.

Looked at within the longer history of the globalization project, Brexit and the policies of President Trump represent an attempt to transform the *terms and conditions* of globalization. But they do not represent an attempt to promote deglobalization and nor are they reminiscent of the catastrophe of the 1930s. Even if the processes that widen and deepen globalization have stalled or partially reversed over the last decade, globalization as a *condition* will be extremely difficult to unravel. The high level of economic and political interdependence within contemporary global capitalism means that the globalized condition is now pervasive. The enormous political difficulties surrounding Brexit, which has proved to be a political problem that overwhelms the capacities of one of the world's longest-standing liberal democracies, demonstrates just how difficult it is to extricate a state's economy from the most intensive forms of economic and political integration associated with globalization.

The crisis of the 1970s demonstrated the capacity of the globalization project to adjust and adapt to significant problems. Ultimately, though, the adjustments made in response to that crisis were not the right ones. They unleashed a more aggressive form of market expansion under the guise of neoliberalism and laid the foundations for a set of ever deeper problems and vulnerabilities within globalization. Similarly, today's emerging national liberalism is an adaptation that does not deal with the underlying problems facing the global economy. Instead, it combines a defence of the economic status quo with an increasingly toxic form of exclusionary nationalism. The globalization project has always maintained some degree of flexibility, but the wrong adjustments have been made. Getting the response right today will require a bigger rethinking of the liberal vision for how to organize the world economy.

Previous crises of globalization can, though, never be more than an imperfect guide to today's problems. History's themes may resonate today but it does not neatly repeat itself. Thinking historically can help us see continuities and differences with previous moments of change and uncertainty. But these patterns do not offer us a blueprint for how to deal with the problems of the present. In the decade that has followed the Global Financial Crisis, underlying tensions within the globalization project have come to the fore once again. But they have done so in new and distinctive ways that present new challenges and require novel political and economic solutions. We cannot simply go back to some supposed golden age of post-war capitalism. And we cannot simply re-embed liberalism in the twenty-first century. We are now living through a critical period of transformation with far-reaching consequences for the future of the world economy and our fate as a species. Reactionary forces have capitalized on the troubled legacy of the financial crisis and they are in the ascendance. If the national liberals continue to shape the agenda of globalization then the consequences will be catastrophic. Deepening climate change will generate widespread human suffering and present a rapidly growing challenge to progressive values of openness, tolerance, solidarity, and cooperation. Border walls will be erected to shut out climate refugees and hostility will be reinforced by a toxic ideology of division. It seems very unlikely that a peaceful international order will survive under these conditions.

Avoiding a dark future will require a coordinated international effort to reset the basis of globalization on a more sustainable and equitable footing. The odds are in many ways stacked against such an effort. The narrow pursuit of national interests is likely to see powerful states and corporations try to shift the burden of adjustment to climate change onto the weakest nations, while minimizing the costs that they themselves have to accept. The fossil fuel industry is able to bring huge financial resources to bear on the political process to deflect attention away from its role in generating climate catastrophe and generate support for pro-carbon politicians. Donald Trump's policies in the United States exemplify this danger.

Combating the tendency towards national self-interest will require an approach based on rediscovering values of cross-border cooperation and solidarity. The neoliberal emphasis on a system of beggar-thy-neighbour competition has proven itself to be intellectually bankrupt and socially and environmentally destructive. We need to nourish the reinvigorated forms of democratic socialist internationalism that are starting to emerge within many different countries. Domestically, progressive political parties will need to harness the energy of civil society and lend their support to the emergence of stronger social movements, working in tandem to transform our economies and prevent the continuation of global warming. Internationally, progressive political parties need to form alliances and seek to harness the power of the state to rebuild their economies in a way that enables a green transition.

There is, though, no avoiding the fact that getting the major powers within the global economy to support this kind of agenda will be crucial. Any international effort to reorganize the global economy on a more just and sustainable basis will require support from the United States, China, India and the EU. In this regard, much will hinge on the 2020 Presidential election in the United States. That election looks set to pit a Democratic candidate supporting the Green New Deal against the threat of a second term for Donald Trump. Another four years of American inaction on climate change will most probably spell the end for any hope of international efforts meeting the targets set at the Paris Climate Agreement. Much will also rest on the relationship between the United States and China. If these two powerhouses of the global economy cannot find a way to work more cooperatively and in pursuit of mutual interests in the face of climate change, then the prospects for salvaging a hospitable planetary environment look dismal.

Global futures

We have seen in the arguments of this book that the deeper condition of contemporary globalization reduces the possibility of its immediate unravelling. So, the good news is that this buys us some time to present alternatives to the neoliberal vision of how to organize the world economy without fearing an immediate return of a 1930s-style scenario of global war and economic disintegration. But the bad news is that the time required to build the movements in support of an international effort to reorganize the rules, goals, and structures of globalization may not be synchronized with the timeframe that needs to be adhered to if we are to prevent the worst effects of global warming. This is a mismatch between political time and environmental time.

What this temporal mismatch means is that the challenge of rethinking globalization is urgent. We cannot escape this crisis by simply reloading a modified vision of carbon-intensive economic growth. Our current crisis represents the exhaustion of the liberal vision of a world economy organized through ever-more specialized and geographically extensive markets that generate unending economic growth. Saving globalization will mean scaling it back in some important respects. Where it makes more environmental sense to produce and consume locally, we will need to do so. Trade and investment rules will need to be supportive of this requirement. But we will also need to scale up our cooperative efforts and mutual support for the transition to a more challenging global climate. We will need to support the movement of people away from those areas worst-affected by climate change. We need less of some parts of globalization and more of others – to change the priorities and purpose of global economic and political interdependence.

Global futures

Whichever way we respond to the challenges of economic stagnation, inequality, and climate change, there is no way of returning to a world before globalization. Our societies and cultures have become too interconnected, our economies too intertwined, and our technologies too advanced to return to the pre-globalized world. Globalization is not over. But it must look very different if it is to survive into the twenty-first century. In the Anthropocene age, whether or not we manage to transform the global economy in a progressive and sustainable direction will shape our trajectory as a species. Securing the right future for globalization is now more than ever also about safeguarding the future of humanity.

Notes

1 The crisis of globalization

1 Rosenberg, J. (2005). Globalization theory: A post mortem. *International Politics*, 42(1), 2–74.
2 Fukuyama, F. (1989). The end of history? *The National Interest*, 16, 3–18.
3 Ohmae, K. (1991). *The borderless world: Power and strategy in the interlinked economy*. New York. Harper Collins.
4 Hirst, P. and Thompson, G. (2002). The future of globalization. *Cooperation and Conflict*, 37(3), 247–65.
5 Robinson, W. I. (2004). *A theory of global capitalism: Production, class, and state in a transnational world*. Baltimore. John Hopkins University Press.
6 Sharma, R. (2016). Globalization as we know it is over – and Brexit is the biggest sign yet. *Guardian*. Available at: https://www.theguardian.com/commentisfree/2016/jul/28/era-globalisation-brexit-eu-britain-economic-frustration.
7 World Bank (2015). Global economic prospects.
8 World Bank (2018). World development indicators, foreign direct investment, net inflows (% of GDP).

9 Helmore, E. (2018). Trump threatens to hit all $505bn of Chinese imports with tariffs. *Guardian*. Available at: https://www.theguardian.com/business/2018/jul/20/donald-trump-tariffs-all-chinese-imports-threat.

10 United Nations (2010). International trade after the economic crisis: Challenges and new opportunities.

11 Peet, R. (2009). *Unholy trinity: the IMF, World Bank and WTO*. Zed Books. London.

12 Costello, S. (2018). Where is the iPhone made?, *Lifewire*. Available at: https://www.lifewire.com/where-is-the-iphone-made-1999503.

13 Wenar, L. (2015). *Blood oil: Tyrants, violence, and the rules that run the world*. Oxford. Oxford University Press.

14 Keynes, J. M. (1919). *The economic consequences of the peace*, pp. 11–12. London. Routledge.

15 Taylor, P. J. (2001). Specification of the world city network. *Geographical Analysis*, 33(2), 181–94.

16 Foreign Affairs (2017). Will economic globalization end? Available at: https://www.foreignaffairs.com/ask-the-experts/2017–06–12/will-economic-globalization-end.

17 Tooze, A. (2018). *Crashed: How a decade of financial crises changed the world*, pp. 144–6. London: Allen Lane.

18 Gamble, A. (2014). *Crisis without end? The unravelling of Western prosperity*, p. 4. Basingstoke. Macmillan.

19 Gamble (2014) *Crisis without end?*

20 Ikenberry, G. J. (2018). The end of liberal international order? *International Affairs*, 94(1), 7–23.

21 Parmar, I. (2018). The US-led liberal order: Imperialism by another name? *International Affairs*, 94(1), 151–72.

22 Sørensen, G. (2011). *A liberal world order in crisis: Choosing between imposition and restraint*. Ithaca. Cornell University Press.

2 Globalization's four liberalisms

1 Tellmann, U. A. (2017). *Life and money: The genealogy of the liberal economy and the displacement of politics*, pp. 4–6. New York. Columbia University Press.

2 Smith, A. (1776). *An inquiry into the nature and causes of the wealth of nations*, p. 456. Metalibri.

3 Smith (1776). *Wealth of Nations*, pp. 14–17.

4 Smith (1776). *Wealth of Nations*, p. 447.

5 Ricardo, D. (1817). *On the principles of political economy and taxation*. Kitchener. Batoche Books.

6 Lacher, H. and Germann, J. (2012). Before hegemony: Britain, free trade, and nineteenth-century world order revisited, p. 116. *International Studies Review*, 14(1), 99–124.

7 Schwartz, H. M. (2009). *States versus markets: The emergence of a global economy*. Basingstoke. Macmillan.

8 Hobson, J. M. (2004). *The Eastern origins of Western civilisation*, pp. 249–50. Cambridge. Cambridge University Press.

9 O'Brien, R. and Williams, M. (2016). *Global political economy: Evolution and dynamics*, p. 67. Basingstoke. Macmillan.

10 Schwartz (2009). *States versus markets*.

11 Hobson (2004). *Eastern origins*, p. 256.

12 Hobson (2004). *Eastern origins*, p. 260.

13 Eichengreen, B. J. (1998). *Globalizing capital: A history of the international monetary system*. Princeton. Princeton University Press. Hume, D. (1882). *The philosophical works of David Hume* (Vol. 2). London. Longmans, Green and Company.

14 Schwartz (2009). *States versus markets*, p. 162.

15 Knafo, S. (2013). *The making of modern finance: Liberal governance and the gold standard*. London. Routledge.

16 Kern, S. (2003). *The culture of time and space, 1880–1918*. Cambridge, MA. Harvard University Press.

17 Mishra, P. (2012). *From the ruins of Empire: The revolt against the West and the remaking of Asia*. London. Penguin.

18 Ruggie, J. G. (1982). International regimes, transactions, and change: Embedded liberalism in the post-war economic order. *International Organization*, 36(2), 379–415.

19 Skidelsky, R. (2010). *Keynes: A very short introduction*, pp. 62–3. Oxford. Oxford University Press.

20 Keynes, J. M. (2018). *The general theory of employment, interest, and money*. London. Springer.

21 Heilbroner, R. L. (2011). *The worldly philosophers: The lives, times and ideas of the great economic thinkers*, pp. 147–52. New York. Simon and Schuster.

22 Skidelsky, R. (1979). The decline of Keynesian politics. In Crouch, C. (ed.) *State and economy in contemporary capitalism*. London. Croom Helm.

23 Blyth, M. (2002). *Great transformations: Economic ideas and institutional change in the twentieth century*, pp. 50–1. Cambridge. Cambridge University Press.

24 Salant, W. (1989). The spread of Keynesian doctrines and practices in the United States. In Hall P. (ed.) *The political power of economic ideas: Keynesianism across nations*, pp. 27–52. New Jersey. Princeton University Press.

25 Sweezy, A. (1972). The Keynesians and government policy, 1933–1939. *The American Economic Review*, 62(1/2), 116–24. Salant (1989). Keynesian doctrines, pp. 37–9.

26 Helleiner, E. (1996). *States and the reemergence of global finance: From Bretton Woods to the 1990s*. Ithaca. Cornell University Press.

27 Eichengreen, B. J. (1998). *Globalizing capital: A history of the international monetary system*. Princeton. Princeton University Press.

28 Frieden, J. A. (2007). *Global capitalism: Its fall and rise in the twentieth century*, p. 17. New York. W. W. Norton and Company.

29 Terborgh, A. G. (2003). The post-war rise of world trade: Does the Bretton Woods System deserve credit? LSE Department of Economic History Working Paper No. 78/03.

30 Helleiner, E. (2014). *Forgotten foundations of Bretton Woods: International development and the making of the postwar order*, p. 2. Ithaca. Cornell University Press.

31 Gowa, J. S. (1983). *Closing the gold window: Domestic politics and the end of Bretton Woods*. Ithaca. Cornell University Press.

32 Frieden (2007). *Global capitalism*.

33 Terborgh (2003). Post-war trade, p. 4.

34 Helleiner (2014). *Forgotten foundations*, pp. 260–7.

35 Maier, C. S. (1977). The politics of productivity: foundations of American international economic policy after World War II. *International Organization*, 31(4), 607–33. Maier, C. S. (2014). Malaise: The crisis of capitalism in the 1970s. In Ferguson, N., Maier, C. S., Manela, E. and Sargent, D. J. (eds.). (2010). *The shock of the global: The 1970s in perspective*. Cambridge, MA. Harvard University Press.

36 Frieden (2007). *Global capitalism*.

37 Peck, J. (2010). *Constructions of neoliberal reason*. Oxford. Oxford University Press.

38 Mirowski, P. and Plehwe, D. (eds.). (2015). *The road from Mont Pelerin*. Cambridge, MA. Harvard University Press.

39 Hayek, F. A. (2001). *The road to serfdom*. London. Taylor and Francis.

40 Hayek, F. A. (2012). *Law, legislation and liberty: A new statement of the liberal principles of justice and political economy*. London. Routledge.

41 Van Horn, R. and Mirowski, P. (2015). The rise of the Chicago School of Economics and the birth of neoliberalism. In Mirowski, P. and Plehwe, D. (eds.). *The road from Mont Pelerin: The making of the neoliberal thought collective*, pp. 139–80. Cambridge, MA. Harvard University Press.

42 Friedman, M. (1962). *Capitalism and freedom: With the assistance of Rose D. Friedman*. Chicago. University of Chicago Press.

43 Friedman, M. (1968). The role of monetary policy. *The American Economic Review*, 58(1), 1–17.

44 Laidler, D. (1981). Monetarism: An interpretation and an assessment. *The Economic Journal*, 91(361), 1–28.

45 Friedman (1968). Role of monetary policy.

46 Friedman, M. (1977). *Inflation and unemployment: The new dimension of politics*. London. Institute of Economic Affairs.

47 Jones, D. S. (2014). *Masters of the universe: Hayek, Friedman, and the birth of neoliberal politics*, pp. 198–9. Princeton. Princeton University Press.

48 Riddell, J. B. (1992). Things fall apart again: Structural adjustment programmes in sub-Saharan Africa. *The Journal of Modern African Studies*, 30(1), 53–68.

49 Peet, R. (2009). *Unholy trinity: The IMF, World Bank and WTO*. London. Zed Books.

50 Schwartz (2009). *States versus markets*, pp. 263–81.

51 Phalguni, S. (2014). An overview of Nike's supply chain and manufacturing strategies. Available at: https://marketrealist.com/2014/12/overview-nikes-supply-chain-manufacturing-strategies.

52 O'Brien, R. and Williams, M. (2013). *Global political economy: Evolution and dynamics*. Basingstoke. Macmillan.

53 World Trade Organization. (20008). *Globalization and Trade*.

54 Scholte, A. J. (2002). Governing global finance. In McGrew, A. and Held, D. *Governing globalization: Power, authority and global governance.* Cambridge, UK. Polity.

55 Slobodian, Q. (2018). *Globalists: The end of empire and the birth of neoliberalism.* Cambridge, MA. Harvard University Press.

56 Gill, S. (1998). European governance and new constitutionalism: economic and monetary union and alternatives to disciplinary neoliberalism in Europe. *New Political Economy*, 3(1), 5–26.

3 Why we are not in the 1930s

1 Carr, E. H. (1981). *The twenty years' crisis: An introduction to the study of international relations.* Basingstoke. Palgrave Macmillan.

2 Schwartz (2009). *States versus markets*, pp. 64–78.

3 Temperley, H. (2002). *Britain and America since Independence*, p. 123. New York. Palgrave Macmillan.

4 Tooze, A. (2015). *The deluge: The Great War, America and the remaking of the global order, 1916–1931*, pp. 355–9. London. Penguin.

5 Eichengreen, B. and Temin, P. (2000). The gold standard and the Great Depression. *Contemporary European History*, 9(2), 183–207.

6 Tooze (2015). *The deluge.*

7 Brendon, P. (2016). *The dark valley: A panorama of the 1930s.* London. Random House.

8 Schwartz (2009). *States versus markets*, pp. 64–78.

9 Tooze, A. (2018). *Crashed: How a decade of financial crises changed the world.* London. Penguin.

10 Bell, D. (2016). *Reordering the world: Essays on liberalism and Empire.* Princeton. Princeton University Press. Mehta, U. S. (2018). *Liberalism and Empire: A study*

in nineteenth-century British liberal thought. Chicago. University of Chicago Press.

11 Gereffi, G., Humphrey, J. and Sturgeon, T. (2005). The governance of global value chains. *Review of International Political Economy*, 12(1), 78–104.

12 Schwartz (2009). *States versus markets*, pp. 219–35; Walmart Company Facts. Available at: https://corporate. walmart.com/newsroom/company-facts.

13 Tooze (2015). *The deluge.*

14 Maier (2010). Malaise, p. 27.

15 Frieden (2007). *Global capitalism.*

16 Hanke, H. J. (2018). World trade returns to the law of the jungle. *Politico*. Available at: https://www.politico.eu/ article/wto-gatt-trade-tariffs-dispute-back-to-gatt-law-of-the-jungle-returns-to-tradeland/.

17 Brewster, R. (2018). Trump is breaking the WTO. Will China want to save it? *The Washington Post*. Available at: https://www.washingtonpost.com/news/monkey-cage/ wp/2018/05/02/trump-is-breaking-the-wto-will-china-wa nt-to-save-it/?utm_term=.003d11fb273c.

18 Laloggia, J. (2018). As new tariffs take hold, more see negative than positive impact for the U.S. Pew Research Center. Available at: http://www.pewresearch.org/fact-tank/2018/07/19/as-new-tariffs-take-hold-more-see-nega tive-than-positive-impact-for-the-u-s/.

19 Slobodian, Q. (2018). You live in Robert Lighthizer's world now. *Foreign Policy*. Available at: https://foreign policy.com/2018/08/06/you-live-in-robert-lighthizers-wo rld-now-trump-trade/.

20 Bhagwati, J. N. and Patrick, H. T. (1990). *Aggressive unilateralism*. Ann Arbor. University of Michigan Press.

21 Morin, R. and Cassella, M. (2018). Trump says no new tariffs against EU after parties agree to trade negotiations. Politico.eu. Available at: https://www.politico.eu/article/

donald-trump-jean-claude-juncker-announces-trade-neg otiations-with-eu/.

22 Morgan, I. (2018). Richard Nixon's opening to China and closing the gold window. *History Today*. Available at: https://www.historytoday.com/history-matters/richard-ni xons-opening-china-and-closing-gold-window.

23 Lambert, L. (2018). Trump threatens to scrap NAFTA in Sunday morning tweet, CNBC. Available at: https://www.cnbc.com/2017/08/27/trump-threatens-to-scrap-na fta-in-sunday-morning-tweet.html.

24 Beattie, A. and Pollti, J. (2018). How is Donald Trump's USMCA trade deal different from Nafta? *The Financial Times*. Available at: https://www.ft.com/content/92e9ce0a-c55f-11e8–bc21–54264d1c4647.

25 Dorn, J. A. (2008). The debt threat: A risk to US–China relations? *The Brown Journal of World Affairs*, 14(2), 151–64.

26 Foroohar, R. (2018). *Globalised business is a US security issue. The Financial Times*. Available at: https://www.ft.com/content/e98ea238–86a5–11e8–96dd-fa565ec559 29.

27 Wu, M. (2016). The China, Inc. challenge to global trade governance. *Harvard International Law Journal*, 57(2), 261–324.

28 Harding, D. (2016). The UK's liberation from the EU demands a global financial investment zone. *The Telegraph*. Available at: https://www.telegraph.co.uk/bu siness/2016/09/23/the-uks-liberation-from-the-eu-deman ds-a-global-financial-invest/.

29 PoliticsHome. (2017). Brexit Britain has potential to be world leader in the liberalization of trade in services – Boris Johnson. *Politics Home*. Available at: https://www.politicshome.com/news/uk/economy/financial-sector/op inion/uk-finance/89562/brexit-britain-has-potential-be-world.

4 Neoliberalism unravelling

1 Milanovic, B. (2012). *Global income inequality by the numbers: In history and now – an overview*. The World Bank. Available at: https://elibrary.worldbank.org/doi/abs/10.1596/1813–9450–6259. Milanovic, B. (2016). *Global inequality: A new approach for the age of globalization*. Cambridge, MA. Harvard University Press.

2 Bourguignon, F. (2017). *The globalization of inequality*. Princeton. Princeton University Press.

3 Borguignon (2017). *Globalization of inequality*.

4 Borguignon (2017). *Globalization of inequality*.

5 Milanovic (2016). *Global inequality*.

6 Gamble (2014). *Crisis without end*.

7 Sharma, R. (2012). Broken BRICS: Why the rest stopped rising. *Foreign Affairs*, 91(2), 2–7.

8 Piketty, T. (2014). *Capital in the twenty-first century*. Cambridge, MA. Harvard University Press.

9 Blyth, M. (2013). *Austerity: The history of a dangerous idea*. Oxford. Oxford University Press.

10 Ostry, J., Prakash, L., Furceri, D. (2016). Neoliberalism: Oversold? *Finance and Development*, 53(2), 38–41. International Monetary Fund.

11 Green, J. and Lavery, S. (2015). The regressive recovery: distribution, inequality and state power in Britain's post-crisis political economy. *New Political Economy*, 20(6), 894–923.

12 Summers, L. H. (2016). The age of secular stagnation. *Foreign Affairs*. Available at: https://www.foreignaffairs.com/articles/united-states/2016–02–15/age-secular-stagnation.

13 Müller, J. W. (2017). *What is populism?*, p. 20. London. Penguin.

14 Müller (2017). *What is populism?*, p. 20.

15 Mair, P. (2013). *Ruling the void: The hollowing of Western democracy*. London. Verso.

16 Slobodian (2018). *Globalists*.

17 Milanovic (2012). *Global income inequality*.

18 Gamble, A. (2001). Neo-Liberalism. *Capital and Class*, 25 (3), 127–34. Krieger, J. (1984). *Reagan, Thatcher and the politics of decline*. Cambridge. Polity.

19 Harmes, A. (2012). The rise of neoliberal nationalism. *Review of International Political Economy*, 19(1), 59–86.

20 Gamble, A. (2018). *Can the centre right survive in Europe? Prospect Magazine*. Available: https://www.prospectmagazine.co.uk/magazine/can-the-centre-right-survive-in-europe.

21 BBC see below.

22 UNHCR (2018). *Refugee crisis in Europe*.

23 BBC (2016). *Migrant crisis: Migration to Europe explained in seven charts*. Bbc.co.uk.

24 Dinas, E., Matakos, K., Xefteris, D., Hangartner, D. (2019). Waking up the golden dawn: Does exposure to the refugee crisis increase support for extreme-right parties? *Political Analysis*. Available at: https://doi.org/10.1017/pan.2018.48.

25 Statista, (2018). Top refugee nationalities arriving in Italy in 2017 and May 2018. Available at: https://www.statista.com/statistics/617712/top-refugee-nationalities-arriving-in-italy/.

26 Newell, L. J. (2018). Understanding the role of immigration in the Italian election result. EUROPP blog LSE. Available at: https://blogs.lse.ac.uk/europpblog/2018/03/12/understanding-the-role-of-immigration-in-the-italian-election-result/.

27 European Parliament (2018). *Integration of refugees in Austria, Germany and Sweden: Comparative analysis*.

28 Habib, H., Embury, D. (2018). Sweden Democrats: Far-right party claims victory despite third-place in general election. *Independent*. Available at: https://www.independent.co.uk/news/world/europe/sweden-democrats-election-exit-poll-latest-social-democratic-party-far-right-moderates-a8530581.html.

29 BBC (2016). Migrant crisis: Migration to Europe explained in seven charts. Available at: https://www.bbc.co.uk/news/world-europe-34131911.

30 Asylum in Europe (2018). Asylum in Germany. Available at: https://www.asylumineurope.org/reports/country/germany/statistics.

31 Taub, A. (2017). What the far right's rise may mean for Germany's future. *New York Times*. Available at: https://www.nytimes.com/2017/09/26/world/europe/germany-far-right-election.html.

32 Haraszti, M. (2015). Behind Viktor Orban's war on refugees in Hungary. *New Perspectives Quarterly*, 32(4), 37–40.

33 Kundnani, H. (2018). Competing visions of Europe are threatening to tear the union apart. *Guardian*. Available at: https://www.theguardian.com/commentisfree/2018/jul/01/three-competing-visions-of-europe-threatening-to-tear-union-apart.

34 Lind, D. (2018). The US has all but slammed the door on Syrian refugees. *Vox*. Available at: https://www.vox.com/2018/4/13/17233856/syria-attack-refugees-war-assad-trump.

35 Inwood, F. J. (2015). Neoliberal racism: The 'Southern Strategy' and the expanding geographies of white supremacy. *Social and Cultural Geography*, 16(4), 407–23.

36 Serwer, A. (2017). The nationalist's delusion. *The Atlantic*. Available at: https://www.theatlantic.com/politics/archive/2017/11/the-nationalists-delusion/546356/.

37 Frey, W. H. (2018). US white population declines and Generation 'Z-plus' is minority white, census shows. *The Brookings Institute*. Available at: https://www.brookings.edu/blog/the-avenue/2018/06/21/us-white-population-declines-and-generation-z-plus-is-minority-white-census-shows/.

38 Blow, M. C. (2018). White extinction anxiety. Available at: *New York Times*. https://www.nytimes.com/2018/06/24/opinion/america-white-extinction.html.

39 Thompson, H. (2017). Inevitability and contingency: The political economy of Brexit. *The British Journal of Politics and International Relations*, 19(3), 434–49.

40 Goodwin, M. and Milazzo, C. (2017). Taking back control? Investigating the role of immigration in the 2016 vote for Brexit. *The British Journal of Politics and International Relations*, 19(3): 450–64.

41 Pirro, A. L. (2014). Populist radical right parties in Central and Eastern Europe: The different context and issues of the prophets of the patria. *Government and Opposition*, 49(4), 600–29.

42 Szczerbiak, A. (2017). Explaining the popularity of Poland's law and justice government. *LSE European Politics and Policy (EUROPP) Blog*, 1–6.

43 Adekoya, R. (2016). Xenophobic, authoritarian – and generous on welfare: How Poland's right rules. *Guardian*. Available at: https://www.theguardian.com/commentisfree/2016/oct/25/poland-right-law-justice-party-europe.

44 Djankov, S. (2015). Hungary under Orban: Can central planning revive its economy? *Peterson Institute for International Economics*. Available at: https://piie.com/publications/policy-briefs/hungary-under-orban-can-central-planning-revive-its-economy.

45 Müller, J. W. (2014). Orban's 'personal leadership', *London Review of Books*, 38(23): 10–14.

46 Ivaldi, G. (2015). Towards the median economic crisis

voter? The new leftist economic agenda of the Front National in France, *French Politics*, 13(4). 346–69.

47 Sandford, A. (2017). What are Marine Le Pen's policies? *Euronews*. Available at: https://www.euronews.com/2017/02/09/what-do-we-know-about-marine-le-pen-s-policies.

48 See: Singham, S. A. and Tylecote, R. (2018). Plan A+ Creating a prosperous post-Brexit UK. *Institute for Economic Affairs*, Discussion Paper 95, 1–131; Walker, P. (2018). PM urged to drop Chequers in order to win 'Brexit prize'. *Guardian*. Available at: https://www.theguardian.com/politics/2018/sep/24/pm-urged-to-drop-chequers-in-order-to-win-brexit-prize.

49 Panitch, L. and Gindin, S. (2018). *The socialist challenge today: Syriza, Sanders, Corbyn*. London. Merlin Press.

50 Leslie, C. (2018). Labour is no longer a broad church. It is intolerant of those who speak their minds. *Guardian*. Available at: https://www.theguardian.com/commentisfree/2018/sep/29/mp-chris-leslie-deselection-threats-momentum-labour-party.

51 Guinan, J. and O'Neil, M. (2018). The institutional turn: Labour's new political economy. *Renewal*, 26(2), 5–16.

52 Guinan and O'Neil (2018). Institutional turn.

53 Partington, R. (2018). How would Labour plan to give workers 10% stake in big firms work? *Guardian*. Available at: https://www.theguardian.com/business/2018/sep/24/how-would-labour-plan-to-give-workers-10–stake-in-big-firms-work.

54 Pearlstein, S. (2016). What Bernie Sanders would do to America. *The Washington Post*. Available at: https://www.washingtonpost.com/news/wonk/wp/2016/03/14/can-bernie-sanders-turn-the-united-states-into-denmark-an-investigation/?noredirect=on&utm_term=.bb7bf3864ba3.

55 Krugman, P. (2019). The economics of soaking the rich.

New York Times. Available at: https://www.nytimes.com /2019/01/05/opinion/alexandria-ocasio-cortez-tax-policy -dance.html.

56 Faris, D. (2018). The incredible transformation. *The Week*. Available at: https://theweek.com/articles/791291/ incredible-transformation-democratic-party.

57 Remnick, D. (2018). Alexandria Ocasio-Cortez's historic win and the future of the Democratic Party. *The New Yorker*. Available at: https://www.newyorker.com/maga zine/2018/07/23/alexandria-ocasio-cortezs-historic-win -and-the-future-of-the-democratic-party; Hess, A. (2018). 29-year-old Alexandria Ocasio-Cortez makes history as the youngest woman ever elected to Congress. *CNBC*. Available at: https://www.cnbc.com/2018/11/06/ alexandria-ocasio-cortez-is-now-the-youngest-woman-el ected-to-congress.html.

58 Haitiwanger, J. (2018). This is the platform that launched Alexandria Ocasio-Cortez, a 29-year-old democratic socialist, to become the youngest woman ever elected to Congress. *Business Insider*. Available at: https://www. businessinsider.com/alexandria-ocasio-cortez-platform- on-the-issues-2018–6?r=US&IR=T.

59 Borosage, R. L. (2018). The ideas primary. *The Nation*. Available at: https://www.thenation.com/article/the-ide as-primary/.

60 Judis, J. B. (2017). The millennials are moving left. *The New Republic*. Available at: https://newrepublic.com/art icle/143239/millennials-moving-left.

61 Spourdalakis, M. (2014). The miraculous rise of the 'Phenomenon SYRIZA'. *International Critical Thought*, 4(3), 354–66.

62 Loomis, E. (2017). A left vision for trade. *Dissent Magazine*. Available at: https://www.dissentmagazine. org/article/left-vision-trade-tpp-isds-international-law.

5 Planning for the Anthropocene

1 Steffen, W., Persson, Å., Deutsch, L., Zalasiewicz, J., Williams, M., Richardson, K. and Molina, M. (2011). The Anthropocene: From global change to planetary stewardship. *Ambio*, 40(7), 739.

2 Skidelsky, R. (1979). The decline of Keynesian politics. in Crouch, C. (ed.) *State and economy in contemporary capitalism*, pp. 55–87. London. Croom Helm.

3 Kindleberger, C. P. (1967). French planning. In *National Economic Planning*, pp. 279–303. Cambridge, MA. NBER.

4 Chang, H. J. (2010). How to 'do' a developmental state: Political, organisational and human resource requirements for the developmental state. In Edigheji, O. (ed.), *Constructing a democratic developmental state in South Africa – Potentials and challenges*, pp. 82–96. Cape Town. Human Science Research Council Press.

5 Johnson, C. (1982). *MITI and the Japanese miracle: The growth of industrial policy: 1925–1975*. Stanford. Stanford University Press.

6 Chang, (2010). How to 'do' a developmental state.

7 Chang, H. J. et al. (1998). Interpreting the Korean crisis. Financial liberalisation, industrial policy and corporate governance. *Cambridge Journal of Economics*, 22(6), 735–46.

8 Wade, R. (2004). *Economic theory and the role of government in East Asian industrialization*. Princeton. Princeton University Press.

9 McKibben, B. (2018). A very grim forecast. *New York Review of Books*. Available at: https://www.nybooks.co m/articles/2018/11/22/global-warming-very-grim-foreca st/.

10 Stiglitz, J. E., Sen, A. and Fitoussi, J. P. (2010). *Mismeasuring our lives: Why GDP doesn't add up*. New York. The New Press.

11 Breslin, S. (2011). 'The 'China model' and the global crisis: From Friedrich List to a Chinese mode of governance?, *International Affairs*, 87(6), 1323–43.

12 McNally, C. (2012). Sino-capitalism: China's reemergence and the international political economy. *World Politics*, 64(4), 741–76.

13 Kearns, J. et al. (2018). China's war on pollution will change the world. *Bloomberg News*. Available at: https://www.bloomberg.com/graphics/2018–china-pollution/.

14 Bal, Y. et al. (2014). The role of China's banking sector in providing green finance, 107, *Duke Environmental Law and Policy Forum*, 24, 89–140.

15 Hilton, I. (2019). How China's big overseas initiative threatens global climate progress. *Yale Environment 360*. Available at: https://e360.yale.edu/features/how-chinas-big-overseas-initiative-threatens-climate-progress.

16 Holden, E. (2018). Trump races against clock to roll back major Obama-era environment rules. *Guardian*. Available at: https://www.theguardian.com/environment/2018/oct/03/trump-administration-roll-back-major-obama-era-environment-policies.

17 Dennis, B. et al. (2018). With a shrinking EPA, Trump delivers on his promise to cut government. *The Washington Post*. Available at: https://www.washingtonpost.com/national/health-science/with-a-shrinking-epa-trump-delivers-on-his-promise-to-cut-government/2018/09/08/6b058f9e-b143-11e8-a20b-5f4f84429666_story.html?utm_term=.ca64e020946d.

18 Milman, O. (2018). Scott Pruitt is out but his impact on the environment will be felt for years. *Guardian*. Available at: https://www.theguardian.com/environment/2018/jul/05/scott-pruitt-epa-impact-on-environment-analysis.

19 Guillen, A. et al. (2018). Trump's environmental policies rule only part of America. *Politico*. Available at: https://

www.politico.com/interactives/2018/trump-environment
al-policies-rollbacks/.

20 Klein, N. (2015). *This changes everything: Capitalism vs.
    the climate*. London. Simon and Schuster.

21 Meyer, R. (2018). The Democratic Party wants to make
    climate policy exciting. *The Atlantic*. Available at: https://
    www.theatlantic.com/science/archive/2018/12/ocasio-cor
    tez-green-new-deal-winning-climate-strategy/576514/.

22 Newell, P. (2018). Labour's low-carbon plan is a good
    start – but a 'green transformation' must go further. *The
    Conversation*. Available at: http://theconversation.com/la
    bours-low-carbon-plan-is-a-good-start-but-a-green-trans
    formation-must-go-further-104052.

23 Murray, J. (2018). Labour vows to be the 'greenest
    government ever'. *Business Green*. Available at: https://
    www.businessgreen.com/bg/news-analysis/3063285/labo
    ur-vows-to-be-the-greenest-government-ever.

24 Alperovitz, G., Williamson, T., Howard, T. (2010). The
    Cleveland Model. *The Nation*. Available at: https://www.
    thenation.com/article/cleveland-model/.

25 Spash, C. L. (2010). The brave new world of carbon
    trading. *New Political Economy*, 15(2), 169–95.

26 Pollin, R. (2018). De-growth vs a Green new deal. *New
    Left Review*, 112: 5–25.

27 IPPC (2018). Global warming of 1.5C: Summary for
    policymakers. Available at: https://www.ipcc.ch/sr
    15/.

28 Dalby, S. and Patterson, M. (2013). Environmental
    politics and the global political economy. In Palan, R.
    (ed.) *Global political economy: Contemporary theories*.
    London. Routledge.

29 Latouche, S. (2009). *Farewell to growth*. Cambridge.
    Polity.

30 Klein, N. (2014). *This changes everything: Capitalism vs.
    the climate*. London. Allen Lane.

6 Global Futures

1 Fogel, B. (2018). Fascism has arrived in Brazil – Jair Bolsonaro's presidency will be worse than you think. *Independent*. Available at: https://www.independent.co.uk/voices/jair-bolsonaro-brazil-election-results-president-fascism-far-right-fernando-haddad-a8606391.html.
2 Phillips, T. (2018). Jair Bolsonaro denies he is a fascist and paints himself as a Brazilian Churchill. *Guardian*. Available at: https://www.theguardian.com/world/2018/oct/30/jair-bolsonaro-denies-he-is-a-fascist-brazilian-churchill.

Index

Index

Index

Index

Index

Index

Index

Index

Index

177

Index

Index

Index

Index

181

Index

Index

Index

Index

Index

Index